Albinism Is *Hot!*

Recognize Your Own Purpose

Cedrick Shamar Lewis

Kingdom Builders Publications LLC

© 2017 Cedrick Shamar

Kingdom Builders Publications, LLC

All rights reserved. No part of this book may be reproduced or transmitted in any form or by any means without written permission from the author.

Printed in the USA

ISBN 978-0-692-90134-2

Library of Congress Control Number 2017944986

Resources

Wikipedia, The Free Encyclopedia.
"Persecution of People with Albinism"
8 March 2013.

N.O.A.H. "What Is Albinism?"
"Social Aspects of Albinism"
1995-2002. Web. 21 March 2013

Authored by
Cedrick Shamar Lewis

Editor
Donald Lee
Louise James

Photographer
JJ Dunlap

Cover Design
LoMar Designs

Albinism is *Hot!*

This Book Belongs to

I wrote this book to inspire albino persons and persons with characteristics of albinism: to build our self-confidence, embrace our beauty, and fearlessly conquer life situations.

~Cedrick

Life is hard and not always fair. No one else can raise your self-esteem.

Albinism is *Hot!*

DEDICATION

I dedicate this book to Mrs. Kaye Houser. Thank you for opening my eyes to see the real world.

CONTENTS

DEDICATION V
ACKNOWLEDGMENTS 1
INTRODUCTION 2
EPIDEMIOLOGY 3
MR. & MRS. LEWIS SPEAKS 4
JERMAINE, HONESTLY SPEAKING 20
TRAVIS HONESTLY SPEAKING 31
DESIREE HONESTLY SPEAKING 45
JASON HONESTLY SPEAKING 53
CEDRICK HONESTLY SPEAKING 66
OUTSIDE SPEAKING IN 76
THE FAM 83
FINAL THOUGHTS 86
THANK YOU 87
FACTS AND KNOWLEDGE OF ALBINISM 88
MORE ABOUT THE AUTHOR 106

ACKNOWLEDGMENTS

I humbly acknowledge my present and former family members.
You gave your thoughts along with open minds. I love you and appreciate everything you offered.

I also acknowledge all persons that were interviewed for this book. You all have help to make this book a complete success.

I am so grateful for the opportunity The University of South Carolina Press provided on this project. Words can't fully describe how appreciative I am of you guys for making my purpose, my dreams a reality. I would rather give the committee huge hugs of appreciation.

INTRODUCTION

Who is Albino? What is Albino? What is Albinism? The word "albinism" refers to a group of inherited conditions.

People with albinism have little or no pigment in their eyes, skin, or hair. They have inherited altered genes that do not make the usual amounts of a pigment called melanin.

Most children with albinism are born to parents who have normal hair, eye color, skin or their ethnic backgrounds. Sometimes people do not recognize that they have albinism.

A common myth is that people with albinism have red eyes. In fact, there are different types of albinism and the amount of pigment in the eyes varies. Although some individuals with albinism have reddish or violet eyes, most have blue eyes.

Some have hazel or brown eyes. However, all forms of albinism are associated with vision problems.

EPIDEMIOLOGY

Albinism affects people of all ethnic backgrounds; its frequency worldwide is estimated to be approximately one in 17,000. Prevalence of the different forms of albinism varies considerably by population, and is highest overall in people of sub-Saharan African descent.

MR. & MRS. LEWIS SPEAKS
Chapter One

Jimmie Sr., born March 4, 1956: a husband, father, and grandfather. To me, he is one of the greatest fathers. Yes, Jimmie, Sr. happens to be my father.

When mentioning my dad to someone, I like to announce him as my father. When saying *"my father,"* I feel the applause because he has done a wonderful job as husband, father, and grandfather. The very same applause goes for my mother — an awesome wife, mother, and grandmother.

Growing up listening to my father tell stories of his childhood, made me realize that he and I are very much alike. He taught me a lot about finding myself and when I've made the discovery, stay true to me, and only be myself; if you will. What I enjoy most with my father is taking those short trips to local stores. We converse about anything that comes to mind. The nuggets in those moments are the ones I value and cherished the most.

When finding the time and the courage to interview my father, it was a challenge and even time consuming. Wednesdays is his days off and he uses that day to attend to his business. He sometimes picks up my mother from work.

Albinism is *Hot!*

    Gladly on the day of his interview, I got up, gathered my tools, and found courage to ask the questions I was apprehensive about asking. When I entered the room where he was seated, he was watching TV. "Let me steal at least an hour and a half of your time," I said. I figured he and I could warm up to tougher questions by conversing the softer and easier lead-ins; such as, *where he was born, how he grew up, and what things he enjoyed doing.*

    My father was the baby boy out of 10 children. His passions were instruments and sports. He really enjoyed the two, but being a percussionist was his absolute favorite. At a young age, his father bought him a drum set, which he played on a regular basis. He played it loudly and clearly on days when he was home alone. He's been a drummer and has been playing for many years. He is now a member of a band called the Precise Band with his oldest son Jermaine and three other members. He also has given me great knowledge of my late grandparents, James and Emma Lewis. I didn't get a chance to meet my grandmother Emma, but for 10 years of my life I enjoyed the presence of my grandfather, James. I can think of many times my brothers, my sister, and I had so much fun with him, especially when he used to playfully chase us with a long, brown stick as we'd get on his nerves. It was a long, thin stick with colored rubber bands tied to both ends: green, blue, red, and tan. He had about three of them that stood up against the door frame.

As my father and I sat and discussed the goals of this project that morning, I was ready to proceed deeper into the interview.

I am so nervous, but here it goes...

In a Q & A session I asked:

Q. Who is Mr. Lewis?

A. *I don't know... I'm me, my own man, a husband, father, grandfather of your stank butt nieces and nephews. Where we are, all of us, I'm happy.*

Q. Tell me about how you met mama. How old were y'all?

A. *I believe I was 26 playing with the band at the park and saw her just looking at me. And I said, "Who is this pretty girl looking at me?" Looking at her, I knew she was younger, like about 16. Time went past and we stayed in the same area of each other, she kept coming around and I started to like her. Her daddy didn't like me at first, but as he and I started talking and I kept coming around he realized that I was a good guy and good for his daughter. I told him he didn't have to worry about Julia, that she'd be in good hands and that I'd take good care of her.*

Even today fathers are the same when it comes to their daughters, wanting to make sure that their daughters are in the right hands of another man. But as for the age difference, it's a whole different scenario.

Q. As you and mama became closer, what made you guys want to have kids?

A. I love kids and wanted to have plenty of them. Your mother wanted the same thing. Though she completed her first year in college, she still wanted to have a big family.

Q. I remember hearing that mama was with child and had a miscarriage. Did that affect you in any way or did it push you and mama to keep trying?

A. It definitely pushed us to keep trying but it didn't affect me or her in any type of way, you know. Things happen.

Q. Yeah. So the second time around, Jimmie Jr. is here. How did that feel?

A. It felt great, my boy here now. Your mama and everybody were happy. Right then I knew what I had to do. Get a job to take care of y'all. I've been working at the City (City of Columbia), for 27 years now, ever since Jermaine was born. We've also gotten married during the same year.

Here is where it gets difficult for me and I became very nervous.

Q. A year later, Travis is here. What were your emotions about his birth and the things that went on after his birth?

A. Well, when he came out I noticed that he looked different and at the same time I know that he and y'all are my buggers. With his eyes, the doctors, your mama, and I wanted to see what the matter of his eyes was and to get him checked out. Later on he went under in surgery and once I talked to the doctors I realized that they were *just experimenting on his eyes and trying to correct the movement of his eyes. I immediately told them to stop before they make things worse for him to see.*

Q. Were you worried of what others would think or say of him? How were you feeling?

A. I know he's mine. I didn't care what somebody else thought or had to say. I know your mama didn't step out on me and we gon' do what we got to do to protect y'all. I'm gon' always be here for all of y'all.

Q. Another year had passed, you have two boys and so now it's time for a girl. You get the girl and now she's here: Desiree. Tell about that experience.

A. Your mama and I both wanted a girl. We were all excited and it just made us want to have another one, another girl. I know she was gon' have the "how they say, pretty eyes like her daddy".

Q. A couple years after, y'all ended up with two more boys. How was that when hoping for another girl?

A. When Jason came we knew we had to recap on some of the things we did for Travis, but no surgery. Then the following year afterwards, you came. What we did for Travis and Jason we did for you; my last two baby boys. After you, your mama said she was finished. I'm glad for all of y'all and I love all of y'all.

We love you, too, Pop!

Let's talk about when mama was sick.

Q. When mama first got sick and you and everyone else started noticing it, what was going through your mind? How were you feeling?

A. *I wanted to get my belt and cut her hip, Acting up like that. But I didn't know. I didn't know what was going on. A lot of people were talking in her ear and she used to take in all of the negative stuff that people used to say to her. So I tried talking to her saying, "You have a husband and children who love you. Don't let anybody outside of this house and family tell you nothing different." My daddy was telling me that she may have gotten sick we were having children too fast — back to back and not letting her body settle and rest. Having one then having one the next year, then another one the next year and so on.*

Q. Did you ever want to leave mama because of her situation?

A. *Nope. I never had any intentions on leaving her. Through sickness and in health I love my wife and all I want to do is help her and take care of her. I know I have a good wife.*

Q. What was the thing you heard that she was told that hurt you?

A. *I was talking to some people and I told them that I didn't want your mama sick like that. I was telling them that I still want her, but I don't want her to be sick. They took what I said and they twisted my words and said to your mama, "Oh, Jimmie said he don't want you no more." I hated that and I hated that I had to explain myself when being questioned about what's going on with me and my wife. She knew people were jealous of her. But for 27 years your mama and I have been going strong.*

Q. Why were they jealous of her?

A. Because she has a husband at home who loves her.

Mm... Amen.

Throughout all the bad my parents went through, the good has always, literally always, outweighed the bad. My parents are the strongest, toughest, and most loving mother and father I've ever met.

Let me introduce you to my mother.

Julia, born November 26, 1965: a wife, mother, grandmother, and again, one of the greatest mothers of all times and yes she happens to be my mother.

My mother is the type of mother who attends and participates in every event — especially when it came to school events that we were in. She was always there. She even became the head parent at the school's PTA meetings. I remember my senior year in high school I was home after school and she said, "I'll be back." As I went to school the next day, all of my teachers were acting kind of different toward me. My last teacher of the day told me that my mother had gone to the PTA meeting the previous night and they could see where I got my respect for others and caring feelings from. They really enjoyed meeting my mother. I felt proud. What I cherish most about my mother are her love and support.

Albinism is *Hot!*

My mother is the middle child out of five children. I never had the privilege of meeting her parents James and Julia Mae Watson, but I did have the pleasure of knowing my great grandmother Daisy Gilmore for 19 years of my life. She was the mother of my grandmother Julia Mae, whom was a very wise woman.

During high school, my mother enjoyed playing the flute and playing volleyball. After graduating high school, she attended college to be a nurse but only completed a year. Because of her love for my father, she put school on hold to start a family.

On a cold and cloudy day around 3 p.m., I said, "Hey, Ma, do you remember the book I was telling you I'm writing and that I want to interview you?"

"*Yeah!*" she said.

And I asked, "Are you ready to be interviewed?"

"*Sure! Come on,*" she said as she and I walked over to the couch. She was so excited. Thinking of the excitement on her face makes me laugh. She was so ready for it, and to see her that happy made me happy and comfortable to ask questions that I was nervous about asking.

Q. All right ... Mrs. Lewis, who are you?

A. *Who am I? I'm a good woman, a wife, a mother, a grandmother. I love going to church and praying for y'all and doing my best to take care of y'all.*

Q. How did you and Pop begin y'all's relationship?

A. We were at the park and he was playing with his band there. And I was just staring at him, with his pretty blue eyes. I knew he was much older than I was but I also knew that I wanted to have him.

Q. After you guys had been together for a while, what made you both want to have children?

A. He and I both wanted children. And when the opportunity and the time was right, we wanted to have a lot of children.

Q. I know you went to college for one year, how was college going for you?

A. Oh it was great; I enjoyed going to school.

Q. What was your course of study?

A. Nursing. I wanted to be a nurse and have a big family.

Q. What made you stop school at that time?

A. I really wanted a family. I felt having a family was more important than my career at the time and I knew that the family was going to be taken care of. We had plenty of good help from family and friends.

Q. As you and Daddy began your family, there was a miscarriage. Tell me how it made you feel as a woman?

A. It was our first child. I was sad, scared, a little upset. I knew that there was nothing wrong with me, and as a woman I thought to myself, "Things happen, let me be strong, and let's keep trying."

Q. You guys tried, and the next pregnancy was a success, which brought Jermaine. How were you feeling after his birth?

A. Oh boy, my baby's here! I was so happy and proud to be a mom. Your daddy and everybody were happy, too. I was looking for the second one.

Q. Then came Travis; tell me about his birth. Was it difficult for you?

A. When Travis came, I along with everyone else noticed how pale his skin was and how white his hair was. The doctors set him under a light to try and darken his skin a little but that didn't help. What was difficult was noticing the movement of his eyes and us trying to figure out how good or bad his eye sight was. When he was a little older he went under surgery and there was nothing that they could do to correct his eyes from the movement and I definitely didn't want anybody playing around y'all and experimenting on y'all. But I figured out what I had to do by asking questions to get y'all to a good eye doctor to get y'all's eyes checked out regularly. And Dr. Christmann was a good doctor, y'all.

Yeah, I liked her a lot.

Q. Now, you have two boys and I know you want a girl.

A. Yep! Desiree.

Q. Did you have any thoughts that she may come out with the same complexion as Travis?

A. *All I've thought was that she is going to look like her daddy, and sure enough she looks just like him; the same pretty eyes and all. I was happy I got my girl.*

Q. I remember hearing that you and daddy wanted another girl and to name her Gabrielle. What was the feeling when you got two boys instead?

A. *Jason was born in 1989 and came out looking just like Travis, I said, "Well, Jimmie, another boy." And we knew what we had to do — take care of him and get his eyes checked too, but no surgery. And then in 1990, you came; another boy looking like Travis and Jason. The same scenario, what we did for Jason and Travis, we did the same for you, and you didn't have any surgery either. But you were the last one and I said no more. I am done.*

Q. Prior to having your children, have you ever seen an albino person before?

A. *Yeah, growing up there was a guy in our neighborhood who was albino and everyone used to pick on him, calling him white, freckle face, and mean things, and I said to everyone else to leave him alone. I've seen his parents and I said he is black just like us. There's nothing wrong with him.*

Q. Do you look back at that moment as a sign that God has blessed you with albino children because you were so humble and nice to him?

A. *Yes, I do. It wasn't easy with y'all growing up, but at the same time, God knew that I would be strong and teach that strength to you, and to let no one run over you, stand with a courage to fight back.*

Albinism is *Hot!*

Here is where I become cold and nervous when asking this question.

Q. A lot of adults I've spoken with say that they've only witnessed seeing no more than one albino person in a household. They also say that we are special, blessed, and that it would be interesting to know all three of us — Travis, Jason, and me — our different personalities. Travis, Jason, and I, especially when growing up, had a hard time trying to express ourselves. We were teased a lot, unaware of who really wanted to be our friends, discriminated by teachers and family members. Seeing the worry that we were going through, how did that make you feel as a mother?

A. I was hurt. My three kids, whom were albino, were constantly picked on. Y'all are black and y'all lived in a black community, so I sent y'all to a predominantly black school. I couldn't be in school with y'all to protect y'all from mean kids and to correct those teachers who were bothering y'all. Seeing the worry on y'all's faces and hearing Travis get into all of those fights was hard to stomach. Seeing all of that together at once, as a mother It broke me down. I became stressed and depressed.

Q. Being stressed and depressed from worrying about us, was that the cause of your illness; your mental illness?

A. Yes. You know, no loving parent to their child wants their child to be teased or picked on. Jason used to come home crying sometimes and I remember your great grandmother telling him that he's a good-looking boy and not to worry about what them kids have to say. And I just used to tell him to tell the kids to kiss his hind parts. You know. Tell them, "Kiss my hind parts."

Let's talk about when you became ill.

Q. When you'd first realized you couldn't take it anymore and you just broke down, how were you feeling and what was going through your mind?

A. It was like it just happened all of a sudden. I knew I was worried about y'all, and you know no parent wants their child or children to be picked on. I worried about how y'all were doing in school and hoping nobody was bothering y'all, and just worrying too much had stressed me out and that's how I became sick. When I went to the doctor, He told Jimmie they were going to put me in a mental hospital. I was aware of everything but at the same time, I knew I needed some help.

Q. Have you ever had any mental issues prior to having children?

A. No, but growing up I used to be very nervous and I used to tremble a lot. Even today, my nerves are still bad.

Q. How has being on medication helped you?

A. I used to not like taking meds, but it has helped me to calm my nerves, I don't tremble as much anymore; doctors told me that I no longer need the medication but I keep taking the meds because it makes me feel better and confident to do what I need throughout everyday life.

Q. During those hard times, did you ever feel that your husband would leave you?

A. Yes, yes I thought he might. I thought he left, and because of those thoughts, I pulled away from him. As I pulled away, he kept coming back, then I realized my husband loves me and he loves our family. Through sickness and health he's going to stand by me. And in realizing that much, I was ready to get well, come home, and be with my family. I'm still standing strong today. And we all go through certain situations in life that we just aren't able to handle. I broke and couldn't handle the stress of worrying every day whether my children are having a good day, mainly at school.

Q. During those times in the hospital, how were you able to maintain your mind?

A. Prayer!

Q. Was it challenging?

A. A little bit. I grew up being in the church and I was a consistent churchgoer. I had all of y'all in church, too. I still go to church regularly today. But as I was in there I prayed and talked to God and he humbled me to be at piece. He helped me to keep my mind, to get well, and to pray for my husband because he's going to be here when I'm ready to come home. I love my husband so much for sticking with me. I prayed for him more than myself or anybody. I knew my children were going to be all right and taken care of.

Q. How do you feel and do you mind sharing your story about your challenges?

A. I don't mind sharing and talking about it. I feel it can help someone who's dealing with stress, depression, or *both, to seek help when need be because we as humans can't handle every situation in our lives alone. I am glad you, my son, are asking questions that can be answered now, because some day, I, your mother, won't be able to give you the correct answers you need. Nobody knows me better than me. I am proud of you. I enjoy talking about it to help you and to help others. I am strong enough to tell my testimony because God has brought me out of many trials to be able to be triumphant today. God is so amazing and so awesome that I truly give him all the praise. Glory to your name, God!*

Oh she's praising Him now ... Go on and dance mama,

My parents, my mother, my father ...

My mother and father, attached or detached, are two of the strongest persons to me. No matter how many trials they've been through, their love for each other has conquered every trial, turning them into triumph. I love my parents, man. They mean so much to me as I mean so much to them.

What I've learned from my parents is how to love and care for myself and others, how to maintain a clean look, how to take care of my body and health, how to be good to myself as well as others, and how to work to get what I want. My needs were always met by my parents, but for the things I wanted I had to work for them, even when it meant working up a fuss with fake tears.

As an adult, I am working ten times harder to make sure that my mother and father are set to relax when entering into their retirement years. It's time that I step out and use the skills my parents taught me: be a man, be tough, and never let anyone tell you, you can't especially when you know you can.

There's no substitute for hard work.

JERMAINE, HONESTLY SPEAKING
Chapter Two

Jimmie Jr., born May 9, 1985, better known as Jermaine to the family and "Snoop" to his friends, the darkest in skin out of the boys, and the oldest of the five of us.

It was great growing up with Jermaine and having him as my oldest brother. He was smart, kind, talented, and always determined for the protection of his brothers and sister. If you'd gotten away with telling ignorant jokes or mostly teasing his brothers without it not getting back to him, lucky you. But if word got back to him, then you were either going to hear a few choice words or feel a couple of hands. He was definitely not shy about slapping someone upside the head. My mother and father taught us well to stick together and to take care of each other. Just like some say, "You mess with one, you mess with all of them."

Today, he's 27-year-old Jermaine, long dreadlocks, muscled, nice-looking guy, and a 2004 Eau Claire High School graduate. He is now a worker at FedEx, the drummer in the Precise Band with our father and three other band members, the father of two handsome children — Amari and Jamiere from a previous relationship — and is now engaged to his fiancée Teresa, whom he's been dating for two years. I really enjoy them two together. It's so funny to hear them crack jokes on each other all in fun. Sometimes I join in.

During the interview process and chatting with my brother, who's eating leftovers: cabbage, rice, baked chicken, macaroni and cheese, and cornbread. We talked at our parents' home, sitting at the dining table while his sons sat outside and played until their mother arrived.

In his Q & A session I asked:

Q. Who is Jermaine?

A. I am me; I try my best to be a better me. A good helper, a hard worker, and a drummer. I am happily engaged and I'm a good father. I love my boys.

Q. Though you were just a baby, one year older than Travis, how did you feel about having a brother?

A. Wow... Looking back, I was happy; very happy to have someone to look after and play with every day.

Q. Did you notice anything different with him?

A. Nope, not at all, just that he's my brother. Of course as we all got older and started school together, people used to pick on him, mainly the students, who would call him white or ask why his eyes move. I just knew I had to step in and defend my brother. I would never let anybody try to bully y'all or speak stupid to y'all. Even today, I'll look at them mean or just tell them to shut up.

At this point, I'm almost in tears. There is nothing like having that love and protection that you need from your family.

Let's talk about the past relationship with the mother of your children.

Q. How and where did you and she meet?

A. She came over here with cousin Keisha and a bunch of other girls, and after mama came and kicked them all out, I went out and hollered at her.

I remember that. I still remember what she had on, too: pink braids and a pink dress. It was cute though. I guess. She was walking down the steps and she said, "She didn't have to kick us out like that." Not knowing she was going to be a part of our lives forever.

But you know, as we started really talking, her mama was saying I'm too old for her daughter and she's too young, she's pressing charges, and all the above madness. But I called her mom one day and started telling her how I really felt about her daughter and how her daughter felt about me.

Daddy always was telling him to leave her alone, but mama said we can't choose his love, and now I bet he wonders, "What if I would have listened to my parents and left her alone?"

Teens can be very stubborn and hard headed.

Q. How old were you?

A. I was 18 and she was 13.

Q. You know, it was shocking to see the transformation of her mother. It really was, to her welcoming the love that you and her daughter shared. And for 7 or 8 long years, did all seem to be going well?

A. Yes! Living in our own apartment, two great kids, working, eating, and place is fully furnished. Then after we broke up, she stole everything from me. Furniture, TV, everything you saw: gone cause she got it. I remember the place looking hot to the max. Cool central air and everything.

Q. How do you feel about the mother of your children now?

A. I hate that bee...autch!

Q. Wow. Why?

A. She know when we were together, I took care of all of us.

Q. Why didn't y'all work out?

A. She was cheating. I come home one morning to find that she's in our bed with another man. So I just didn't want to be with her anymore. When you don't want to be with that person anymore, but that person still wants to be with you, that person tends to spaz out and do dumb crap like put you on child support and try to make you out to be the bad person.

All right! In my opinion, child support can be a stupid ploy only for ignorant and selfish women who use the system inappropriately. Some women knew he didn't have much when you she laid down with him. What are you thinking?... that within 9 months to a year it's going to change some men? Men and women, you made it, take care of it. If you can't get along, no you don't have to be together. But sit down and have some sense about co-parenting your child or children.

Key words...some women, some men.

Q. What are the conversations like when talking to her?

A. At some point in there she's always finding something to argue about. It's making me mad just thinking about it.

Q. What made you and her want to have kids?

A. I wanted mama and daddy to have and see some grandkids. She and I discussed it and so we started sneaking and having sex in each other's parent's homes.

Hmmm, you know I do remember hearing somebody having relations in the closet. I'm in my room listening to music as usual, my brothers room is right across the hall and so I turned down my radio to only hear what I thought I was hearing which were moaning hums to loud thumps on the wall. I thought to myself, how disgusting. but good. Get it anywhere you can get it. The reason they were having relations in the closet was because my brothers took their beds down to make their bedroom a recording studio. So the only soft spot they could use was in the closet on a pile of clothes.

Q. Now she's pregnant. Did you have any thoughts that the child who would be coming out might be albino? And how old were you?

A. You know I didn't care. I was just happy to see my son. But she and her side of the family were talking, "What if he comes out albino looking like his brothers?" I didn't say anything; I just kept it to myself. I have two handsome boys and I love them both. I was 21 with Amari and 23 with Jamiere.

Q. Looking back on that relationship, do you regret anything?

A. Nope. But I've learned that you can't always be nice to someone, because they will take advantage of you and your family. When her mother put her and our child out of their house and our mom and dad took her in, fed her, gave her a place to sleep and wash, they just forget all of what we did for them. But I'm not worried. What goes around comes back around. And like I said, I love my boys and I do what I can for them.

Q. Are you paying child support?

A. Yes.

Q. How do you feel? Are you happy?

A. I'm good, I'm straight. I would feel better if I had a better job and not having to pay child support.

I had to ask...

Q. Is there any chance of you and her getting back together?

A. HELL NO!

Enough said.

Well, let's get to know her.

Kia is a 23-year-old independent mother of four children, a hard worker who is pursuing a degree in mortuary at Gupton-Jones College of Mortuary Science in Decatur, Georgia.

I'm not friends with Kia on the social network site Facebook. So after one minute of searching for her, I immediately sent her an e-mail:

I am writing a book ... (Albinism Is Hot!) I would like to speak with you and ask you a few questions mainly about our family and would like for you to be as open as possible, if you are willing to contribute your thoughts.

It's okay if you're not open to it.

But if so, please call me or we could chat here.

After 3 days, there were no replies so I said, "Jermaine, what's them boys' mama's number? I'ma call her later tonight."

Later tonight is here and after a brief update on both of us, and her wishing me success on the book, I re-explained everything about the book and she and I were up and ready to talk.

I replied again to "please be as open and as honest as possible."

I started by asking:

Q. Who is Kia?

A. *An independent mother of four, working hard to support my kids, thriving to make their lives better, giving them more out of life, and living well.*

Q. How do you feel?

A. *I feel good; I am happy.*

Q. Cool. Tell me about the first albino person you've ever seen or are my brothers and I the first albinos you've ever seen?

A. *Yes! You, Travis, and Jason are the first I've ever seen.*

Q. What did you think? What were your reactions to seeing us?

A. *I thought y'all were adopted, y'all look white, and I just thought it was so different. One day at school, I curiously asked my biology teacher like, what is it? What's the difference between an albino human and a normal human?*

Adopted ... Let's talk about you and Jermaine ...

Q. How did you and Jermaine meet?

A. *We met at your parents' house. I was 13 and he was 18 and we just took it from there.*

Q. I remember your mother strongly disagreeing about y'all's relationship. What did you think made her change her mind? Did you ever ask what the big, sudden change was?

A. Yeah, she didn't agree with that relationship at all at first. She wanted to press charges and everything and I was like, "No, I love him, don't do it." But I guess she started to realize, "No matter what I say, she is still going to run off and be with him anyway."

Q. What made you and Jermaine want to have kids? And how old were you when you had your kids?

A. I was 17 when I had Amari, still in high school, and 19 with Jamiere. But he and I talked about it, and then Amari kind of came unexpectedly.

Mmmhm...

Q. How are your other two kids, the twins?

A. Oh they're good.

Her twins are from a relationship after my brother.

Q. With your oldest son, were you concerned about the appearance of Amari, whether he'd turn out albino?

A. Inside, I knew that there was a chance that my son could have been albino because it's in Jimmie's (Jermaine's) genes. I felt the same during my pregnancy with our second child Jamiere. I kind of wanted to experience what your mom went through with having my own albino child.

You can't sort of experience that type of heat. You have to get burned involving all or nothing.

Amari is 6 years old, he likes school and having fun while playing his drum set. Jamiere, is 4 years old, he likes school and playing with all of his toys. Neither of the two shows any signs or symptoms of albinism.

Q. Speaking of my mother, what are your thoughts of my mother?

A. Uhhh, she's a nice person. I thought she never liked me and I think she's bipolar. One minute she's like, "Hey, hi, how are you?" Then the next minute she's cursing me out and want to fight me or something.

Mmmhm ...

Q. Did you learn anything from the Lewis family?

A. From Mrs. Lewis, I've learned a lot. Mr. Lewis always kept quiet, stayed in the room because he knew the type of wife he has when there are other girls living in the home. And from the family, y'all are good people. Everyone is for themselves and did y'all own thing, and when it's time to come together y'all know how to come together and have a good time.

Q. Did you learn anything from Jermaine?

A. I've learned what type of woman I am and the type of man I want to know and be with. My past with Jermaine, I do not regret.

I don't know why I'm asking this ...

Q. Do you see anything in the future with Jermaine?

A. About us being together, uh, no.

Fine with me.

Anyway! Here's my take on Jermaine and Kia:

Do you know when you meet someone for the first or second time, and you say to yourself, "I don't like them," and you just can't figure out why? But then you sit back and observe as time progresses, you get to see who they are and the type of person they become. It's scary in some type of way.

As I watched these two and their relationship, I have learned that if you do not converse with each other while expressing the way you feel about each other, how are you going to maintain a healthy relationship, whether they are together or not, while co-parenting children? You both are never going to agree on things, your children will begin to ask their 'why' questions, and I hope as responsible parents, you both will answer your children with open and honest answers.

I wish I could use the fire that's within me to burn the pages of my flaming thoughts. But I have grown from that era.

Honesty is still the best policy.

TRAVIS HONESTLY SPEAKING
Chapter Three

Travis was born August 9, 1986. His friends call him Trab a.k.a. "Hook Man." The surprisingly super light-skinned one is now known to be an albino and he is the next to the oldest brother.

Growing up with my older brother Travis, I've seen him do lots of creative things with his hands. One day after school, he and I were sitting at the kitchen table while doing our homework and I glanced over to see what he was doing. He was drawing a girl using basic shapes; a round head, long rectangular limbs, with a triangular skirt. I was so amazed and inspired by it that I started drawing my own and never stopped from then on. I am now more skilled in drawing female dolls. Today, my dolls are inspired by fashion trends today.

I have watched him take apart plenty of items and put them back together; such as VHS videotapes, phones, desktop and laptop computers, TVs; you name it. I am sure he can fix the situation.

My brother these days is a homebody. He's tall, buffed, talented, and intelligent. He enjoys spending most of his time in his room making music beats, expressing the way he feels about his struggles in life. He is a 2005 graduate of A. C. Flore High School. To me, the guy is hilarious in everything he does. He does the Insanity Workout video and I have to admit that it works very well for him. He likes action and animated movies and spending quality time with his love, Destiny.

She is now a graduate of Midlands Technical College with an associate degree in science. She wants to be veterinarian. I like Destiny; she is so cool and so funny to be around. Destiny, Travis, and I always eat and watch movies together as we crack jokes on each other. Travis also is the father of his gorgeous daughter, Egypt, whom he had from a previous relationship.

Travis is the first brother in this family to have albinism. When he was born, I'm sure it might have been a shock to our parents and perhaps even the doctors to see a child to come out of his mother's womb with less pigmentation.

As Travis, Jason, and I grew a little older, our parents and doctors started noticing movement in our eyes which was obviously shifting or shaking back and forth and from side to side. That symptom is called Nystagmus: regular horizontal back and forth movement of the eyes. Jason and I have never had a surgical procedure for our eyes but, Travis was the only one of us to receive surgery on his eyes. Today we now know that the nystagmus of the eyes cannot be corrected. It's caused by misrouting of nerves from the eyes to the brain.

Surgery will not improve eyesight. During the process of his surgery, our dad found out that the doctors were only interns who were experimenting on his son's eyes. Immediately he called off any future surgeries before anything could have gotten worse. In the meantime, Mama found us an excellent eye doctor, Dr. Linda Christmann, MD Pediatric Ophthalmology, who thoroughly examined us as toddlers until our early to mid-teens. Due to the surgery that Travis once had, he sees well with his head faced forward but often turns his head slightly to the left to see what he really needs to see. He says he sees better with his left eye than his right eye. According to the doctor, Travis is legally blind and that glasses and treatment do not help in making him see things far away. In my experience, he can drive, day and night with help from the passenger in reading signs that he can't see. He also has had jobs. But due to transportation issues he was unable to keep the jobs. It's the same scenario when applying for colleges. Not everyone is comfortable with taking classes online. Some prefer being inside of a classroom. He wants to maintain a career as a computer technician.

At some point when we were still babies, our mother applied for Travis, Jason, and I to receive Social Security Income from the government. Travis's SSI was constantly cutting on and off, receiving it then not receiving it. Mama is still fighting for his disability claims.

The same day after my interview with Jermaine, Travis was willing to share his thoughts while he and I drank an ice cold straw-ber-rita drink. Months prior to the interview he'd always say he would need a drink to get motivated before doing any interview just to talk with me.

Indeed it helped.

During the interview I asked:

Q. Who is Travis?

A. *I'm a father, I enjoy making music, I'm loving, kind-hearted. Sometimes I feel like I don't do anything right, but I do. I ask a lot of questions just to be sure of some things I do.*

Q. As you've gotten older and started to realize your differences, how did you feel? Did you have any questions?

A. *I felt different from everyone else around me. I asked why I'm this color, why do my eyes hurt, and when I had surgery on my eyes it seemed like they messed my damn eyes up.*

Q. When you started school, what type of student were you?

A. *At first I started being bad for attention. I thought no one liked me or wanted to be around me. I was always sad or mad when people teased me, calling me white or just staring at me.*

Q. How were you treated by teachers?

A. *Teachers thought that I needed this tremendous amount of help. But I didn't. I appreciated it but I've managed a lot on my own.*

Q. Still in school but outside of class, you, Jason, and I had to work with Mrs. Kaye Houser, lead teacher of the vision impairment and Mr. David Atkinson, orientation and mobility instructor, who are teachers at the Richland County Schools District One. Excellent teachers, by the way. How did you feel about receiving their help?

A. *I felt forced to receive all of this help that I felt I didn't need. I felt that my opinion of it didn't matter to anyone. Mama and Daddy just told me to be good and to accept the help when people really want to help you. Sometimes, I enjoyed the walks with Mr. Atkinson downtown. They are great people to work with and are good to the family.*

Aww man, they are awesome teachers. Mrs. Houser was like our school mom and didn't let any students or teachers cross us the wrong way. Some teachers and students thought that they were our parents anyway. I have to admit that having them pick us up from our classrooms was embarrassing.

Q. Have any teachers teased you?
A. Yes.

Q. Tell me about that. What happened?
A. All I remember is that he pushed me. And it wasn't anything playful about it. I was ready to go home and tell my dad, and when I did, My dad went up to the school and set the teacher straight. Dad told him if he ever put his hands on me again, there was going to be NO talking next time.

I know that's right!

Q. When our sister and your two baby brothers were born, how were you feeling about yourself?
A. I felt odd at first when being the first middle child — seeing that my brother is brown-skinned, my sister is brown-skinned and I'm the only one that's so pale and light. When you and Jason were born I started to feel stronger and motivated to have someone else in the family to go through my similar struggles with me.

Q. When did you start to gain your own confidence in yourself?
A. People showed me how great I am at what I do and how much of a cool dude I am. It made me come out of my shell. I also had a lot of friends and females that wanted to be my friend or girlfriend, or both, telling me how cute, fine and handsome I am!

Q. Why do you always wear that stocking cap on your head?

A. I feel comfortable with wearing my stocking cap. I always wore something on my head. Not hiding myself or anything, I just always felt comfortable with wearing something on my head.

As long as I can remember he always wore something on his head ever since high school — sweatbands, do rags, hats, stocking caps.

Q. How do you feel about yourself and what's going on in your life?
A. I feel good. I feel relieved about some things that are no longer bothering me in my life. I'm not happy about having my daughter in the middle of her mother and me. We have our mishaps, but we seem to be managing, co-parenting Egypt well.

Let's talk about your past relationship with Egypt's mother.
Q. But first, how do you feel about your daughter being around boyfriends of her mother?
A. I feel all right, just treat her right and don't put their hands on her in any type of way. Talk to me and let me handle my daughter.

Real Talk ...

Q. How and where did you meet her?
A. I met her at one of my homies' house. She seemed to want to talk to one of them, but when she saw me, she started coming around more and I knew she wanted to talk to me. She came to our house and then our relationship began there.

Q. During the year or so when y'all were together, how did you feel about her?

A. *I loved her; I really loved her. I believed I found my soul mate.*

These two were like Velcro. They always were together and I've never seen two people who love each other so much that they act just like each other. I enjoyed them together and they were hilarious together.

Q. What made you guys have a baby?

A. *At the time, I felt she was the one just for me. I loved her, she loved me, so we agreed to have a child.*

Q. If you can remember, where was Egypt conceived?

A. *I believe at her mom's house.*

Ohhh!!!

Q. Do you like her mother?

A. *Nope. Only because I know she never liked me, but I respect her. I think she was jealous of her daughter's relationship with me, especially seeing her daughter happy with a good man while she was still single.*

I don't think that she even tried to get to know you. Anyway.

Q. Time passed, Skyye is pregnant. During the pregnancy, how were you feeling about the chance of your daughter coming out an albino?

A. *No matter what, I knew that she was going to be beautiful. And she is... Egypt looks just like her mom with the same complexion and all. I love my daughter and I will always be in her life. Egypt is four years old and is a character. She has always made me laugh ever since she was a few months old. My little loud and sensitive princess. She is very sweet. She really enjoys school and kicking butt in karate classes.*

Q. How did Skyye's mother feel about you, her daughter and the pregnancy?

A. Well you know she doesn't like me. She got mad with Skyye, so for spite, she kicked her out of the house, and started saying hurtful things like: "I hope y'all's baby come out crazy, have mental problems, be badly ill," crazy crap like that. After that, I just didn't want anything else to do with her mama.

She needs to go somewhere and sit down IN SEVERAL SEATS with all that bull crap. Some people just say the dumbest things to hurt you and feel no signs of sorrow behind it. Pitiful.

Q. How come you and the mother of your daughter are no longer together?

A. I felt that she couldn't handle my advice. I would tell her to do right, go back and finish high school, let's be together with our daughter; move out, find our own place and not live off our parents. She thought I was trying to control her, or be her daddy but, I just wanted what was best for us, start a new life together. But what really drove us apart was the drinking. She and I both drank, but she drank a little more than me. We would fight; literally fist fight and argue. She started cheating and that was just the last straw for me.

I remember hearing several nights of them arguing and fighting. The majority of the times, it was funny. Gladly they didn't physically scar each other. I also remember hearing several days and nights of them doing it — bed banging up against the wall ...

Q. How do you feel about her?
A. She's all right. She just keeps making stupid decisions sometimes; like this dumb crap of asking me to be put on child support. I told her if she ever do that to me, when she knows I take care of my daughter, she won't ever have to worry about seeing me or saying crap else to me. Just let me see my baby.

Real Talk ...

Q. Is she a good mother to Egypt?
A. She's a great mother. She does well with her.
Q. Would you and Skyye ever get back together?
A. No! Hell no.

I wonder what makes them say hell no ...
Here's Skyye:

Skyye is 22 years old, a mother, hard worker, and is now embracing her independence.

A month prior to talking to Travis, I called Skyye to ask her to participate in this book. We updated ourselves on each other, she wished me well, and was happy to contribute her side of the story.

I mentioned being as open and as honest as possible is crucial ...

In her Q and A, I asked:

Q. Who are you?

A. I'm a mother, a worker, I love my independence with my daughter and I'm a person who likes to have fun.

Q. Cool. Tell me about the first albino you've seen or met? Are Travis, Jason, and I the first albinos you'd ever seen? What did you feel, say, or think?

A. No, The first albino person I'd seen was actually a girl with red eyes. I didn't think much of it, even after I noticed her red eyes. I just thought, different. I didn't feel afraid or anything.

Wow. Red eyes. Honestly, seeing that would have frightened me a little.

Q. When you first met Travis, what was your first thought?

A. I thought he is so fine, sexy. We started talking for a while then I've realized that he has such a kind heart. I still care for him and I couldn't have chosen anyone better to be Egypt's father.

Q. What are your mother's thoughts on Travis and also the family?

A. She said he's different, nice looking, and a nice guy. She said you all are kind-hearted people, but crazy.

Mmmhm ...

Q. How was it when you met the family?

A. Aww, man. Y'all are so much fun, crazy entertaining. You guys can argue but then nip it the bud and show love to each other only minutes after the argument is over. Now that's family love.

Let's talk about your pregnancy.

Q. What made you and Travis have a baby?

A. *I loved him, we loved each other, and I felt he was the one, so I thought, "Sure, let's have a child."*

Q. What if she had come out as an albino?

A. *That wasn't my concern. I just wanted her to be healthy. I knew she was going to be so beautiful and talented. Come on, look at Travis and me. My mother, she just wondered what if, but it wasn't a huge concern of ours.*

I'm sure everyone was eager to see their baby and see her skin complexion. Egypt does not have any signs or symptoms of albinism.

Q. How were you feeling after you became a mother?

A. *I was like, "Wow, this is my baby, I have a baby, I'm a mom and she is going to be calling me mom for the rest of my life." I sort of wanted a boy, but I love my little princess. Travis was so happy that she's a girl.*

Q. Are you glad that she's not albino?

A. *Yes, but I don't care. I don't feel any type of way about it. I just don't think that I could've handled the stress of seeing her sad and down from being teased.*

Let's speak on you and Travis.

Q. Do you feel some type of way now that Travis is happy with someone else?

A. *I feel a little jealous because I do miss my fun times being there with the family — joking, eating, watching movies.*

Q. Why didn't you and Travis work out?

A. *We are two strong-headed people. I wanted to do my own thing. I was too stubborn to take his advice and work things out, so we eventually parted ways while co-parenting.*

Q. Did you realize what you were getting yourself into when dealing with his challenges, such as having to drive him everywhere, due to legal blindness which caused him to be unable to receive a driver's license?

A. *I didn't mind at all. I loved him and loved taking care of him.*

Love conquers all ...

Tell me about you and my parents.

Q. What did you think of my parents?

A. *Strong couple. Mrs. Lewis is so soft and sweet and bitter when need be and Mr. Lewis is so quiet and sweet as well.*

Q. What have you learned from my mom and the family?

A. *From your mom, I learned how to cook that macaroni and cheese, from the family; how to love, how to argue then bounce back with love.*

Q. Just thinking, was your mother jealous of your relationship with Travis?

A. *Sometimes I thought so, but I didn't care.*

Q. Is there a chance in the future for y'all getting back together?

A. *I don't know. I never thought much about it.*

Mmmhm ...

Albinism is *Hot!*

Travis and Skyye:

Aww, man! These two were so compatible. I thought they would never slip apart, they were like Velcro together. I honestly miss fun moments joking around with them.

But when these two start arguing, they do not or cannot come to an agreement. I've heard them say some of the stupidest, craziest, and most hilarious stuff ever heard in an argument before. I remember plenty of nights literally laughing myself to sleep hearing them argue all night.

Travis is hilarious to me. Let me tell you a story about him. We used to have this red car our father bought for the family. One day, we were all wondering, who took the car and where was Travis? Remind you, he does not have a driver's license, but sure enough, Travis took the car, showing off with his homeboys. He got in a car accident. He arrived home with no harm from the accident. He told us he was in an accident. "Where did they hit you," we asked? "They hit me in the back." "Oh, okay," we said. "We can see the dent. We also see a dent in the front of the car. How did a dent get in the front?" Travis says, "They hit me then ran, so I chased them down and hit them back." My family and I laughed so hard that day, but Daddy did not think that was funny, not even a bit.

But what I've learned from them is that you have to watch what you do and how you say things to each other when you're a couple, especially two strong-minded people. Situations and words can easily be twisted for the bad.

Kind words cost little but accomplish much.

DESIREE HONESTLY SPEAKING
Chapter Four

Desiree was born August 2, 1987. *"Pretty Eyes,"* is what they call her, our only sister, who used to be a tomboy and the third middle child.

Growing up with my sister, I know her most as being very outspoken. She would definitely speak whatever is on her mind. I guess that's what some would expect from her, since she's the only girl of five children. I think she is rude, demanding, but sweet. She's tough, but doesn't mind helping others and shedding a few tears every once in a while. I also remember her being a huge lover of dolls and I really enjoyed how talented she was when coming up with these amazing stories and gathering up all of those dolls of different colors and nationalities and combining them as a huge family of one. I used to have fun with the dolls as well. She used to buy the Barbies and the Baby Barbies, I used to buy the Ken dolls and action figure dolls to make the Barbies have boyfriends and husbands and the Baby Barbies to have fathers. I love reminiscing on those moments because the stories were amazingly funny and very entertaining.

Yes I used to play with dolls and I enjoyed every moment of it.

My sister Desiree is a very beautiful woman, a C.A. Johnson High School graduate. She's the type of girl who looks great with long hair or a nice short haircut — petite, nice body shape with hips that everyone notices and adores, and she is very talented. She is gifted with the use of her hands when doing hair and caring for the elderly. She is a certified nursing assistant and enjoys being a mother of her two-year-old daughter, Journei. I am sure that she would love to have another little one soon. But I must say that until I'd watched Journei, I'd never before seen a daughter grow up to look just like her mother right before my eyes — the very spitting image.

While explaining this project and interviewing her for the first time, she didn't want to tell any of her life's stories or have anything juicy to talk about, whether it was about herself or her brothers. I said to myself that this is going to be a tough one.

My sister always has something to say about someone else, but when the tables are turned her mouth is sealed with Super Glue.

Here's a little something that I was finally able to grab from my sister after multiple attempts to interview her.

Q. So Desiree, tell me about you, who are you?
A. I'm a certified nursing assistant, a single mother of one, and I love being a mom.

Q. How do you feel about being a single mother? Are there any difficult moments?
A. No, I love being a mother. Single or not, I enjoy motherhood. Journei is very well taken care of and when she or I need something from her father, he always provides it for us.

Q. That's good. How did you guys hook up?
A. Well, he'd been after me for a very long time you know, since he'd been friends with Jermaine. And after a while, I decided to give him a chance. We started talking, then we began to mess around.

Q. When you found out that you were pregnant, did you want to be, and were you ready?
A. I was happy and I knew soon I would want a child. I

was a little nervous, it's my first child and all you think about is the feeling of being pregnant, the birth, and then taking care of your child. I knew, no matter what, she's going to be taken care of and be alright.

Q. Jermaine and Travis had their children with no signs or symptoms of albinism. Did you have any thoughts or concerns that Journei would appear to be albino?
A. *No, I didn't think about it at all, it wasn't a huge thing for me. My brothers are albino and y'all are just fine: very creative, talented, and lots of fun to be around. And if Journei happened to have been albino I'm sure that she would've been as beautiful as she is now.*

Journei is two years old and is a bunch of sugar, full of energy. She enjoys acting, singing, and dancing. She's also very talkative and is definitely not shy about opening up to give you a show and being herself around anyone. Have you ever had a complete conversation with a two year old? Journei has no signs or symptoms of albinism.

Q. Growing up, how did you feel about your brothers being albino with you at home or in public?
A. *I didn't feel anything because y'all are my brothers, you know. And at school or in public in general, nobody has ever come to me and asked me questions about y'all. Never, but those who know us always ask for y'all and they want to know what you, Jason, and*

Travis are up to.

Q. Cool. So how is Desiree now? How are you feeling?
A. *Oh, I'm well. I'm living well in my own home, I'm a proud mother loving my child, and I'm working hard to support us both.*
Q. Do you think that you and Journei's father will get back together?
A. *No, probably not.*

I told you guys it was going to be like pulling teeth, getting anything out of her, but I can assure you that the way some things are going in her life, I see in the distance, there will be lots of drama in the future. I'll keep you posted.

Let me introduce you to Journei's father...

As I interviewed my brothers and their ex-girlfriends and wife, it was only right that I interview my sister's ex-boyfriend.

When contacting him through Facebook, I explained this project and he replied back by saying, "OK."

I said to myself, "He's not going to call me. I don't even know if I should wait for him." But, three weeks later, when he called, I felt like that was the call of my life. I also felt that now this chapter would be complete.

Here is Chaun:

Chaun is a hard worker, working two jobs to support himself, his daughter, Journei, and his other child from a previous relationship. Chaun has been close to the Lewis family for many years.

Q. Hey, what's up man, what's going on?
A. Not much, man, just steady working. I'm actually on break right now but we can talk.

Q. Cool, man, thanks for keeping me in mind. Okay, I want to start by asking, who you are and tell me a little about yourself.
A. Well, I'm Chaun, I'm a hard worker. I love to work, especially now that I have responsibilities to attend to and I want to make sure that the people I'm involved with are taken care of. Now, a little about me, I used to be a troubled kid. I always wanted to be different. I've always been that way. I guess that was the cause of my bad behavior. Being different for me was behaving in a bad manner. My mother and I both look and act alike. Sometimes, she and I couldn't stand each other and would not get along. As I've got older, I chose some paths and got myself into some situations that I could readily get out of, I realized my attitude and behavior had to change. I am now more mature. I take great care of my kids, and the relationship I have with my kids' mother ... Man, we are tighter than ever. I tell my mama everything and she gives me good advice to follow.

That's awesome man. I'm glad he found that out at a young age, that he is responsible for himself and his other responsibilities.

Q. Tell me, how did you meet Desiree?

A. I went to school with Jermaine and one day when I saw your sister, I tried my hardest to get to her and get to know her, man. I'm telling you right then and there I fell in love with her.

Q. Oh, wow. So when y'all started to talk, who came to whom?

A. After years had passed she made it clear that she wanted to talk to me and, man, I was so happy. I was like, Yes! I finally got her!"

Let's speed up and talk about 2010. Desiree's pregnant.

Q. Tell me about how you felt when you heard Desiree was pregnant.

A. Aww, man, I was so excited — so excited that my daughter is mine from a woman I've always loved and wanted to be with. I love my daughter, too. She has her mother's eyes, but she looks just like me.

Q. Why didn't things work out between you and Desiree?

A. I guess I just wasn't the man she thought I was and she just didn't want to be with me. I'm the type of guy who wants to get married and have a family. I want to come home from work to a wife and kids, but it'll happen one day.

Sure thing.

Q. Being that my brothers and I are albino, did you have any thoughts that it's possible that Journei could have come out being albino or having

albinism?

A. Oh, that was the last thing on my mind. I just wanted my baby girl. Watching y'all deal with the albinism; y'all are good. You carry yourselves very well.

Q. Are my brothers and I the first albinos that you've ever seen?

A. Yeah, Initially, I didn't know if y'all were white or black. But I know now. You guys are just like us, regular black people and gifted. You guys have the gift to stand out and be different naturally.

I have never heard anyone describe my brothers and me, or any albino person, in that way before. Now that's different for me.

Q. How do you feel about the Lewis family?

A. The Lewis family, man, y'all are cool. From Mr. and Mrs. Lewis down to you, the baby boy, y'all are real cool to be around and for anyone to get to know. Y'all know how to stick by each other. And whenever you guys need me, I'll be there to help out. Even before Journei was born, y'all have always been like a family to me.

I really appreciate that.

Q. Do you think that there's a future between you and Desiree?

A. Umm, if she's willing to change and work things out, then I just might reconsider how I feel.

I still didn't get the full story ... but it's cool. I'm glad that Chaun was able to contribute his thoughts to this project. He also made it feel complete.

Desiree and Chaun:

There isn't much I can say about these two, because I don't know anything! What I *can* say is, communicating respectfully with each other is everything and it means a lot. Learning how to co-parent is the right way to handle these types of situations. Each side has to respectfully cope with other relationships with other people. Just have the child or children in a safe environment. Children are meant to grow up in a home with a mother and father. If that can't be the case, respect each other enough to share your children. It takes two to make a baby. Why is only one parent in the picture? Is it a necessary reason?

Good people build their lives of a foundation of respect.

JASON HONESTLY SPEAKING
Chapter Five

Jason was born April 3, 1989. J–BO is what his friends call him, the other albino brother, and the first baby boy.

Oh my goodness. Jason, Jason, Jason! What can I say about his crazy, lovable butt? A party is definitely not a party if Byron (Jason) isn't there.

Because Jason and I are the last two baby boys, we've experienced a lot together. When we were growing up together; a year apart, people always thought we were twins. While attending school with Jason, I saw him as very friendly, outgoing, and athletic. Basketball was his sport, receiving trophies and awards for good behavior, outstanding achievements. He had great self-confidence and he had a way with the girls. I have to admit, I was a little jealous of his swag. He's always having good things going for himself: a great job right out of high school and working his way up to the supervisor position, a nice apartment he shared with his wife now, providing for his own — a decent living.

Jason is a 2007 C.A. Johnson graduate as well. He's tall, with a swimmer's build, and has dreads. He is married and is stationed in El Paso, Texas, with his soldier wife, Brittany. They're living what I call, *The Army Love Life*. I just knew it. It was bound to happen for them to get married. They'd been dating for about ten years. It was destined. I know they are happy and enjoying each other.

After Desiree was born, two years later came Jason, the second brother, who is also albino, in this family. My mother and father were prepared and knew exactly what to do: regular checkups and regular examinations, nothing extra. His eyes have the same nystagmus, just like Travis', with his eyes shaking back and forth from side to side. Jason hasn't had any surgery on his eyes, just the regular monthly checkup — retinoscopy, refraction, eye cover test, slit lamp examination, glaucoma test, visual field test, and dilation. In spite of our lack of good eyesight, our vision did not interfere with our performance in school or our field of work.

A few months after speaking with the rest of my family, Jason was the last. I called him around 9 p.m. and explained to him and his wife about this project. It was about 7 p.m. central standard time in El Paso, Texas, to our eastern standard time and 9 p.m. in Columbia. Brittany, Jason, and I chatted for about three hours.

As the interview began, I asked:

Q. All right, you ready?
A. Yep.
Q. You need a drink, Vodka, Gin, Hennessey? (with lots of laughter)
A. No, I'm good!

Cause he just had a bottle an hour ago! Just kidding.

Albinism is *Hot!*

Q. Okay. Today, who is Jason?
A. I'm a husband, an uncle, a great person. I love to have fun, love being around people and having fun.

Q. How is it, living in El Paso?
A. Aww, man it's hot. It feels and looks like the desert. No trees, no grass, my front yard is filled with dirt and rocks, !

Q. Dang! Do you go outside?
A. No, I just stay in the house during the day. Sometimes it gets up to 110 degrees in the summer.

Q. Wow. How's Brittany? I'm going to talk to her as well.
A. She's doing well.

I always get a little nervous with my brothers when asking them questions such as the following one:

Q. Great. Tell me about when you were growing up and started to realize that some things are quite different about you. How were you feeling?
A. I felt odd around other people, especially in school. I was feeling that no one wanted to really be my friend and I hated it when they just stared at me.

Q. How do you feel when people stare at you now? Do you get angry or upset?
A. Sometimes it doesn't really bother me, and other times I just want to say, "What the hell you are looking at?"

Q. Have you ever said that to someone?
A. Yes.

Q. What did they do or say?
A. They didn't say anything, just walked away.

Q. Okay. How do you feel about being albino?

A. It's all good, you know. I just wish I had better eyes to see well, but overall I like who I am. I love myself.

Q. What do you like about it?

A. It's different, I'm different. I like different. I'm just glad I'm not crispy black, though!

Q. (with laughter) True! Have you ever thought about why you aren't the same complexion as Mommy and Daddy, Jermaine and Desiree?

A. Yeah, I thought about it and, at times, I asked why I came out this way, but it's all good now. I love the way I look.

Q. Awesome. When someone calls you a name like "white boy," or so, how did or do you go about hearing that and how do you respond when people ask you why does your eyes move like that?

A. I don't feel anything or do anything. I just can't stand when someone stares at me. That bothers me the most. I hope they know that they'd better not put their hands on me. You know what I'm saying? I don't play that. Say what you want, just don't put your hands on me. Respect me.

Q. That's right. Are you confident in yourself?

A. Yep, always.

Let's talk a little about school and having to work with Mr. Atkinson and Mrs. Houser.

Q. How did you feel about school?

A. School's all right. We all need that general education, our diploma.

Q. Yep. How were you feeling when having to work with Mr. Atkinson and Mrs. Houser?

A. I felt like, "Why? You know. I'm good. I don't need this help. I can manage on my own." But as I think back on it, the help from them was greatly appreciated. You know. When someone is willing to help you, let them help you. Even when you think you don't need the help, it's good to know that somebody has your back.

Yeah. I miss them though.

Q. As they used to come up to the school and once a week and get us out of class or call us down to the front office or library, were you ashamed of them?
A. I was embarrassed — especially when the students used to ask, "Is that your mama? Is that your daddy?"

Yes, I experienced that as well. I just told them, "No." But they were like our school mom and dad though! Yes indeed.

Q. While working with Mr. Atkinson and Mrs. Houser, what did they have you to do every once a week with them?
A. Working with Mrs. Houser, we just stayed on school campus, classrooms, or the library. We did vision tests by looking at shapes and numbers from distance, cutting out shapes on the black borderline, with or without borderline, checked my hearing and graded my reading level skills and was a great help when I needed extra help with my school work. With Mr. Atkinson, we mostly did a lot of walking, mainly downtown.

Travis and I practically encountered the same thing.

Let's talk about life after high school.

Q. So, 2007, you've graduated high school and received your diploma. How do you feel now about the choices you've made?

A. Well I knew I wasn't going to college; I've always said that. I struggled with high school. I used to cut school with my homey, Tony, riding around with him, smoking, drinking, and chillin,' you know. I didn't like school. I was just glad that I was able to get a good job working at Fort Jackson as a DFA (dining room facility attendant). Within a year, I became a supervisor. Wow!!! I've done that for a while but I came down from the supervisor position because I don't like being the one having to fire someone.

Q. How long have you been working there altogether?

A. Three years.

Let's speak a little on when you moved out.

Q. When you moved out, I was happy; happy for you that you were growing and becoming your own man. I was happy to have my own room, but there was some jealousy in me because I was feeling, "OK, if he can do it at his age, then so can I." How do you feel about knowing I had some jealousy towards you?

A. No, man, I just feel like you shouldn't have felt that way at all. I mean, I know you were in college but, you could have gotten a job working with me. You could have gotten out the house and leased your own apartment.

I wasn't prepared to be on my own yet, I only wanted it because you and Jermaine had it.

You know you can do anything you want.

(Smiling) Yeah.

Let's talk about you and your wife.

Q. What's your story on how you guys met?
A. *Well, we met at a house party and she was stalking me, you know (laughter)! As a little time passed, we started talking and getting to know each other and things just went on good from there.*

I remember when I first saw Brittany, when she came to our house. She had on this cinnamon-colored wig and a black denim dress with heels back in summer of 2004. When I answered the door, I asked, "Who is it?" "Brittany," she said. As I opened the door, she leaned her head to the side, flipped her hair out her face and said, "Is Jason home?" (I said to myself, "OK, where's she going!?") I replied, "Yes, he's here. Come in."

How can I best describe these two, Hmmm, "Crazy In Love" with arguments, fussing and fighting, drinking — just a whole lot of "Life, Love & Sex."

Life: These two stuck by each other's side, no matter how much whomever disagreed with their relationship.

Love: These fools fight and argue and make up every time. I pay them no mind.

Sex: Sex had to have been what kept these two together. Sex brings a bond to a relationship that pushes both mates to fall in love.

When these two were living with the family and me in our parents' home — to my knowledge — there was always arguing, fighting, sex, arguing, fighting, sex, sex, sex, and more sex. Don't get me wrong, there is nothing wrong with sex. It's amazing, and I'm sure everyone enjoys it, especially when used to come closer in a relationship, and all of that is cool. It's just messed up that I had to share my bedroom with that mess. Some thought I was jealous of their relationship and their behavior, but hell no, ! I just was perturbed of how disrespectful they were while sharing the bedroom. No hard feelings; it's all love. Get it anywhere you can get it.

Shoot! I would have done it myself!

Anyway!!!

Q. So after all you guys have been through, y'all decided to become as one. Tell me how the marriage came about.
A. Well, as she was getting into the army, we talked about it. I didn't feel ready, but I said, "Why not? We've been together and loving each other for so long. Let's do it, let's make it happen." We got married November 14, 2011, in Virginia.
Q. I remember when you came from Virginia and told us you were married and would be leaving for Texas in February of 2012. Mama and Daddy were proud and crying, we were happy and surprised.

When you guys come back home, I hope we can throw y'all another full wedding with family and friends, because I want to be a part of somebody's wedding! Do you mind?

A. *No I don't, but yeah, we're going to do something soon.*

I see a great future with these two. Sometime soon I hope to see a baby or three from them. When the time is right and whatever they decide to do together, I support them 100% and I love both of them.

Now! Let me introduce Brittany:

After Jason and I finished our conversation, we told each other we love each other and he handed the phone over to Brittany.

Brittany is 24 years old, from Columbia, South Carolina, signed to the U. S. Army 92W, Fort Jackson Army Base South Carolina, Oct 10, 2010 to present. She became a Soldier in 2011. Currently, she is assigned to 3/1 125 BSB, U. S. Army 92W, Fort Bliss Army Base, El Paso, Texas, Dec 2, 2011 to present. She is also pursuing a business degree at the University of Phoenix.

Q. Hey, Brittany. How are you?

A. *Hey. I'm good.*

Q. How is life in El Paso?

A. *It's good, you know, we're doing what we've got to do.*

Q. Yeah. Tell me about yourself. Who are you today?

A. Aww, man! That's a story all by itself right there! I'm a woman with a troubled past, as I'm still growing, I try my best to remain a positive person. I'm a wife and struggling soldier. It's not as easy as some people make it out to be.

Q. Tell me about that life, the army life. Do you like it?

A. Yeah, I like it. In the army, most people expect for the man or your husband to be in my position but my husband does what's best for him and I'm grateful for my husband.

Q. How did marriage come about for you two? How do you like being married?

A. It was like a tug of war. He asked, I asked, we felt that it was about time but, "Are we serious for marriage?" and "Is this the right thing to do?" So here we are, married. I love it. We were engaged for 4 months in 2011.

Q. Will there be any children in the future?

A. Soon as I receive a steady job, there will be some running around.

Awesome. Let's rewind it back to the beginning of you guys' relationship.

Q. How did you guys meet?

A. We met at a house party and we've gotten to know each other, we decided to pursue our relationship.

Q. When you first saw Jason, what did you think?

Was he the first albino you've ever seen?
A. When I first saw him I was like, "Where is his color?" At the same time, I was curious about knowing more about him. I didn't pay any attention to his eyes, the movement of them until later on. I was already in love with him. He was just so nice and sweet.

Q. Aww. How was your family feeling about Jason after having met him for the first time? What did they think of his appearance?
A. Everyone one was cool. My niece, when she was younger, was scared of him. But as time passed, she just couldn't get enough of Jason — always asking me, "Where is Jason, where is Jason? When is Jason coming over?"

Let's talk about driving with Jason.

Q. Though I have experienced riding in the car while Jason was driving, my experience wasn't that great. Do you let him drive for practice sometimes? How were you feeling in the beginning when you realized you'd have to drive him everywhere?

A. No I don't let him drive, but what do you do when he just takes the car? But I love him and it's my duty to take care of him and keep him happy.

Let's speak a little on my family.

Q. How do you feel about this family?

A. Y'all are great people, very kind hearted. Y'all have plenty of personalities and know how to combine them all together as one bundle of joy. And stepping into a *family who has 3 albinos is so cool and so interesting. You, Travis, and Jason somehow make people want to get to know y'all. You are all well-kept with good looks and charm.*

Q. You've been in the family the longest out of any of the companions. Have you learned anything from the family?

A. You know from Mr. Lewis to Mrs. Lewis, Jermaine to you and even down to the nieces and nephews, y'all know how to love. Strong love, tough love, silly love, crazy love. I've experienced it all with you guys and I've learned how to handle those types of loves. No matter what y'all go through, at the end of the day, the love y'all have for each other mends the bond back together. I am blessed to be a part of this life and this family.

Jason and Brittany:

I don't even know where to begin with these two. They have fire that the Brazilians; they argue like little rug rats, they fight worse than cats and dogs, but know how to kiss and make up with some hot and sweaty sex. Ugh, I can't believe I just said that. I just hated having to share a room with that mess.

But what I have learned from these two is how to be a go-getter. They envisioned where they wanted to be; and made every attempt to reach out and get there. The army, marriage, and El Paso, Texas.

Every child has to become an adult, branching out and making one's own decisions, whether they are good decisions or bad ones. We have to make our own mistakes, recognize them and then correct them.

I wish them the best of luck out there with many prayers. We all miss you guys here at home, where you both are always welcomed.

You have to give up something to get something.

CEDRICK HONESTLY SPEAKING
Chapter Six

I, Cedrick, was born August 6, 1990. Ced or Ceddie-Ced is what they call me, the last one who's albino, the last baby boy, and also labeled as "the *weird* one."

Just as with Travis and Jason, my mother and father were prepared once again and knew exactly what to do: regular checkups and regular examinations — nothing extra. My eyes have the same nystagmus as theirs, eyes shaking back and forth from side to side. I have also not had any surgeries on my eyes, just the regular monthly checkup — retinoscopy, refraction, eye cover test, slit lamp examination, glaucoma test, visual field test, and dilation.

Growing up, I always tried my best to grasp a crowd to fit myself into while trying to be myself. That was actually extremely hard for me because I wasn't behaving as myself. I wanted the bright and cool personality as my brothers had back in our school days. Gosh, as I look back on it, I was so weird: quiet, talked and I cut up with some associates and friends but not too much.

I stayed to myself mostly in school and at home. I kept myself entertained by having dreams and desires of being in the entertainment world. I drew pictures of women in fine clothing because I desired to be a fashion designer. I tried to break into that business in the easy way, but there is no easy way. I enjoyed singing and dancing and I still do, even modeling. I know I am not that great of a singer, but I do have potential to make a hit! Look at some of the artists today. I was glad that I was able to find myself and become my own man, finding my own style right after high school.

After graduating from C.A. Johnson, in 2008, I did not attend college right away. I got stuck, not knowing direction for my future. In 2009, I attended a community college for eight months. That did not help me enough to maintain a career in an office setting, so the following year, I landed my first job ever as a receiving clerk at Walmart for six months. I really hated the work. In August of 2011, I got a job working at the South Carolina State Museum, maintaining retail, wholesale, and marketing and went back to a technical college majoring in marketing. Sadly in 2012, I was laid off because a project for the museum called the Body Worlds Vital exhibit had ended. While not performing well in college, I decided to put school on hold the same year. I realized that marketing isn't something that I wanted as a career however I will always have knowledge of marketing strategies.

During that hard time, I continued to look for any type of work; except restaurants. I do not like working at restaurants. But while looking for jobs day in and day out, I realized that actually became my new job; looking for a job. I would wake up, seek jobs online or go door to door. At the end of the day, I was exhausted. I gave up plenty of times on trying to find jobs but have always bounced back to continue job hunting. The year 2012 began to fade after many years of asking and praying to God, "What is my purpose in life? Why am I here? What am I meant to do for you?" My prayers have truly been answered.

Today I am a 22-year-old, cute, close-cut pretty boy. I am single and thriving to be successful, to gain my own independence. I'm not rushing it, just taking it one day at a time. Currently, I am working at the University of South Carolina bookstore, selling books. I like it and I enjoy it, but not exactly the career choice that I am seeking. But I absolutely know and see where God is taking me, enabling me to succeed in my goals.

After interviewing everyone else, it was guaranteed that I would interview myself. One late night until the early morning, I was so determined to finish my chapter, because I knew that this was going to be a long night of strong thoughts and deep feelings.

All right! Let's get it started.

Q. Cedrick, who are you?
A. At the moment I'm a homebody during the day. I would love to be working somewhere. And since I have put school on hold, I have never felt boredom this bad. Anyone can sit around and be poor. I'm not going to be that person.

Q. Tell me about your struggles with finding yourself and, accepting who you are. How was that difficult for you?
A. I am the baby, the last child, and for many years things have been given to me. I've always gotten what I wanted. Because of being so babied, I had problems with growing up and doing certain things on my own. I figured if I acted like my brothers I would be cool just as they are.

Q. Who pampered you the most?
A. Umm, everybody, actually: mother, father, my siblings, teachers, some friends. But in the words of my mentor, Mrs. Houser, "A cute face will only get you but so far." When I was 17, she taught me that I had to work, and work hard to get where I want to be, and earn me place in the world.

Q. Before following in the footsteps of your brothers, what was your individual character like?
A. I was childish. As I look back on those moments, I hate the way I acted. I mimicked my brother's acts, trying to build my own character or fit in with my brothers; I looked like a childish fool. I really hate flashbacks of those days.

Q. So, when did you begin to feel comfortable with your character?
A. Right after graduating high school. Indeed it was the perfect time for me because a new stage in life was beginning for me.

Let's talk deeper about your looks.

Q. How do you feel about your appearance?
A. I like it. It's different and I like different.

Q. Living in an African American environment, do you wish to be a darker skin-toned?
A. Yes. I wish my skin was a little more tanned with sandy brown hair. I love the color of my eyes, but I wish I had 20/20 vision.

Q. How bad or how well can you see?
A. I can't see things too well from afar. But I can see well enough to enjoy life and do many things on my own with this disability.

Q. Are you and your brothers legally blind?

A. In the words of doctors, yes, but that doesn't determine what my brothers and I can or can't do. My brother Travis drives, remember, and he had surgery on his eyes.

Q. Do you think surgery helped his vision?

A. No. I believe my brothers' vision and my vision are about the same.

Q. What were things like for you in school?

A. I loved school and enjoyed going. But the teasing and finger pointing sometimes made me dislike everything about school, especially when some students would be so cruel to other students who aren't African American or at least look close to being Black.

Q. How were you feeling every week at school? What was going through your mind?

A. I knew waking up for school that, OK, I could look forward to another day of finger pointing and name calling. I felt that I would feel better if I had gone to an international school, mostly filled with Caucasians. I was happy that I was able to gain friends throughout my time in general education and that some students calmed down from being so ignorant about the appearance of others.

Q. Have any teachers treated you differently?

A. Yes. Some teachers showed me less favoritism than the other students.

Q. Could you tell me about a time where a teacher paid you no attention?

A. I would raise my hand to read aloud or would know an answer to a question, but I would be the last person the teacher would ask or I would hardly ever get picked at all.

Q. How were you handling those moments?
A. *I brushed it off. I paid it no mind and I knew I was smart.*

Tell me about working with Mrs. Houser and Mr. Atkinson.

Q. How were you feeling about the help of your mentors?
A. *I don't remember how they came about. I just knew that I didn't want the help and definitely did not want to be teased or laughed at anymore. It was embarrassing and tiring being asked by students if they were our parents. You tell them "no" but they still would ask again and again just being funny about it. But now that I am an adult, I greatly appreciate their help. When I'm out walking or riding my bike I think of things Mr. Atkinson taught me. When it comes to school and handling business, I think of things Mrs. Houser taught me. I use all of their information to the best of my ability.*

During my spare time I really enjoy visiting Mrs. Houser. I'll bet she doesn't know that just being in her presence makes me want to keep striving for perfection.

Speaking of striving for perfection, you've worked very hard on this project. What made you write this book?

A. *After finishing high school I began to fully get to know God for myself. And while doing so, I asked Him: "What is my purpose?" On November 2012, He answered my prayers. I really enjoy watching celebrity interviews on my laptop. One afternoon, as usual, I was watching celeb interviews with The Breakfast Club @ Power 105.1, on YouTube. The hosts were interviewing an albino rapper by the name of Krondon from the west coast rap group called Strong Arm Steady.*

One of the hosts asked the rapper, "Last time that you were here, you walked outside and said that sun was bothering you. You had a hoody on. We know that you are albino. Explain what an albino person is." The rapper said, "I would love to share light on that because a lot of people are ignorant to what albinism is." And as he went deeper into the subject, he schooled the interviewers with knowledge of albinos with symptoms of albinism. Immediately after watching 25 minutes of the complete video, God dropped in my spirit to write a book. I really heard God say, "Write a book." I prayed and meditated on it. When God gives you something you have to take it and run with it. It is for the good of your own well-being. I am grateful He chose me to do this project.

They say when you're constantly thinking of a goal that you just can't get out of your head, it's best that you go ahead and achieve that goal. Goals are dreams with deadlines.

Q. Was it hard to put together?
A. The concept and the title came easy to me. Gladly my interviewees were willing to contribute their thoughts. I am also thankful to have positive praises about an unfinished project. The hard part came when putting the pieces together.
Q. Why did you proceed with writing this book?

A. I would like to help build the self-confidence of persons with albinism, persons with disabilities, and people in general of all nationalities. This book also explains that albinos are humans and we go through life situations just as any other human does. I believe this will be amazing. This is one of many amazing books.

Q. Tell me how you are feeling now. What's going through your mind?
A. I am happy. I am very excited to be attending to my goals every day, seeing them to completion. I enjoy being a steady worker.

Q. What's your motivation?
A. Wow. I have numerous things that keep me motivated, but I keep in the back of my mind the words of Mrs. Houser, "I don't think you know what you are getting yourself into. You don't have any idea how big this is going to be for you." That pushes me to stay up through late nights and early mornings, constantly writing.

I really love writing and I know that this is the right career choice for me.

Q. Do you like encouraging others?
A. I love encouraging others.

Q. Which encouraging moment do you remember the most?
A. I used to work at Walmart. While working there I once saw an African American mother and father with their daughter who has albinism. I was walking and glancing through the aisles and I walked past them at first, then I stepped back and walked down the aisle

just to see their daughter and I said, "Hey." I knelt down to the girl and said, "You are so beautiful." She looked like she was about 6 or 7 years old. She looked at me, held her head down, and lightly shook her head like she wanted to say thank you. Her mother was in tears and her father smiled and said, "Thanks, man," while shaking my hand. I then asked them if I could help them with anything. That moment is still very precious to me.

Cedrick: I realized I come across to some people as a guy who doesn't know much, or doesn't know how to step outside the box. I am very aware of life and some of the ignorant people who come with it. Yes, I'm a spoiled child. I guess at 22 I'm too immature for some people, and I don't have a car and my own place. For me at age 22, that's fun time. Time to plan out my life and career and be mature when need be. What I have come to realize about myself, and others with albinism is being albino is like being gay, black or white.

Albinism is not something that you are. I'm a black man who came from two African American parents who gave birth three children with albinism. We came out white but our diagnosis is better known as albino. My brothers and I are black or African Americans with albinism.

Being albino and having characteristics of albinism are very hard. There are a lot of stressful moments that you think about. You hope people really want to be your friend and accept who you are. You wonder who's going to help you as you get older or why you have to be stared down like you're some type of species or what we're called the most — aliens. It's hard when you walk into a room full of black folks with different shades of color and people single you out as the whitest black person in the room. That is stressful and always embarrassing for me. Becoming an adult, I have learned how to cope with myself. Some people may call me cocky or arrogant, but I know that it's built-up confidence I've gained from looking at myself and encouraging myself. I know that I'm handsome and I am willing to go outside the box to be somebody with great success.

Successful people don't find time—they make time.

OUTSIDE SPEAKING IN
Chapter Seven

When seeing certain types of albinos and persons with different stages of albinism for the first time, I am sure that there's a little fear and there are questions that you really want to ask them, such as, "Are you white, black, biracial?" "How did you come out like this if both of your parents are black?" "Are you blind or why do your eyes move like that?" Now does that sound like nice questions to ask someone, especially in front of crowds of people? I cannot even count the amount of times I've been embarrassed or had my feelings hurt, or both.

We albinos are human, and just like any other human, we have feelings. No more asking us sensitive questions out loud in the midst of crowds, embarrassing us or you just might find yourself embarrassed.

In this chapter I have listed mini interviews with persons outside of my family's home. I've included comments from family members who have known us forever, friends who have been in our lives for a while, and a few random persons to get their insight on my family and on any albino person they have seen before seeing members of my family or me.

Thoughts on the Lewis Family and General Albinism:

"When meeting Travis, Jason, and Cedrick for the first time, I said, 'Aren't they the cutest ones' ever?' and that 'they're mine and I'm going to work with them.' I really enjoyed and it was my pleasure to work with these three young men and watch them grow. They are all interesting and different and there is something about them that makes you want to get to know them and be around them. They are unforgettable. Before fully working with the boys I've done some research on albinism. The research has helped know what to teach them and how to work with them to make sure they are getting the help they need while in school. Mr. and Mrs. Lewis are wonderful parents and have raised beautiful children. I love the Lewis family."

- **Kaye Houser,** *Richland One, Lead Teacher of the Vision Impaired*

"The first albinos I've ever seen were you and your brothers because I grew up with you guys. ! I never thought that y'all were weird or different in any type of way. I treated y'all like any other family member. Our family comes in different shapes, sizes, and colors. That's what makes our family so unique."

-**Shante' Cantlow,** *Cosmetologist*

"I actually have albino cousins on both my mother's and father's side of the family. So all my life I've been around albino people. I actually like albino people. Even though I look at everyone equally, I do know that they are very unique. I'm jealous of their eyeballs, , because mine are brown and boring while theirs constantly change colors. I still really never looked at albinos any differently, and if anybody does I would think it'll be in a good way. All the ones I know are just as cool, if not cooler than the average person. I notice every day how my albino cousins get all the girls, ! They are talented and funny as hell. So that's a plus. Albinos are the 'Shiz-Nitz.' What more can I say? ! I love my Lewis side of the family. I don't see them as often as I would like to, but when I do I feel like we never skipped a beat.

Very welcoming, nice, caring, loving, generous family. Never ever a bad memory or thought. In spite of not spending much time with them, it's not a day that goes by that I don't pray and thank God for my family as a whole because I am who I am today because of them. When it comes to family, I consider myself beyond blessed."

-Ricky Golston, *college student*

"When seeing my first albino person I thought to myself, "What is wrong with him? Why is this guy so pale, why his hair so bleached blonde or what did he do to himself? I had many questions this guy so different, as far as his looks? I hadn't gotten to know him because he was just another customer in my store. He was very friendly but he never looked me directly in the eyes. He slightly kept his head down. I don't know anyone who's albino, personally, but I do believe that they are regular humans as me and anyone else. Albinos are people who lack pigmentation in their skin, I found out as I researched information on albino persons. And the customer who came in my store was a nice-looking albino man, not like the weird and funny looking ones they have displayed online."

-Michael Blusher, *Clothing Store Owner*

"I believe Cedrick is the first albino person I've ever seen. At first, I couldn't tell if he was light skin or white. But I am so glad that I have gotten to know him. He and I have known each other for a very long time and he and his family are beautiful people from their looks to their personalities."

-Tiara Jennings, *college student*

"The first albino person I've seen was at a family reunion 1985, on my father's side of the family. And when I saw her, I immediately was horrified of how pale she was and the movement of her eyes. I tried not to stare but I was so curious about where she came from and how she felt being the lightest person out here in the midst of all of these African and Latin American people. When the reunion was over, I decided to talk to my mother about it and she said that Sheena, the albino girl, is my cousin from my aunt and uncle, and that she just doesn't have pigment in her skin to make her look black as we do. But she's black, honey. After my mother told me that, I thought, "Cool," and I was curious to know more about albinos. And now that I do know more, I see that albinos are in every nationality and a lot of them are smart and talented in various ways."

-**Mark Borelli,** *Science Professor*

"Cedrick, Jason, and Travis are the first albino persons I've seen and gotten to know. The look of them, I thought, was interesting, different, and new to me. One day I decided to do some research on albinos or albinism. And what I read was very intriguing. Research has drawn me closer to being friends with Cedrick and his wonderful family. With knowing them, it has made me feel good to have him as my friend to explain his condition to other friends of mine when they meet him."

-**Kiara Richardson,** *college student*

"When I first saw Cedrick, I thought, 'What is wrong with him?' I have never seen anyone else who looked like him before. But as we grew up together, I learned that he is very funny, smart, encouraging, and talented. He's always there when I need a friend to talk to. It is obvious that he'd come from a warm and loving family. He portrays it very well."

-**Raven Brown,** *college student*

"I don't remember the first albino I saw. When I see an albino person I feel that they are normal people and they should be treated the same way as other people who are not albinos. The color of a person's skin should not matter and all people should be treated equally. I know albinos are cool, friendly, very outgoing, and talented. I love the Lewis family very much and I treat them as my own family. I treat all of them like my brothers and sisters. All of you have your own personalities and are unique in different ways. I love all of you, and Mama and Daddy, too."

-Brittney Truick, *college student*

"I saw my first albino person back in college and she always kept to herself. I guess no one thought to give her a chance to break out of her shell. But you, Cedrick, are the first albino person that I've gotten to know and you are pretty cool and outgoing with a lot of confidence in yourself. While working with you, I've realized that you are talented, smart, and know what you want out of life at a young age. You're the man. Ced, make the world proud of you."

-Leonard Plaski, *Film Director*

"Jason and Cedrick Lewis. I didn't feel any different towards them. First thoughts were 'they must be mixed' and I wondered why their eyes moved the way they do. I have only had the pleasure of interacting with a few albinos and I love them like family. The Lewis family is very loving, kind-hearted people who are funny and outgoing."

-LaQuita Jones, *Personal Care Aide*

"The first albino person I met was you and your brothers when we were younger. I didn't understand what albino was. I just thought I had white cousins. As far as how I felt, I didn't understand what albino was. I didn't really care for you guys'

Albinism is *Hot!*

color because y'all are my family. I just loved playing with y'all at Granddaddy Lewis' house when we were younger. Today I don't see albinos as different people because I have albinos in my family. I think they are unique because they have no pigment. I used to wonder why their eyes shake, but now I know because they're sensitive to light. Sometimes I feel sorry for them because their skin makes them super sensitive to the sun. I wonder how they really enjoy life, 'Can they comfortably go to the beach, or do they have to wear a million clothes, sunscreen, and shades?' I don't treat them differently and can't stand people who do. I don't know if it's because I have albino family members or if I just hate people being treated differently in general. As far as the Lewis family, I love them. They are family even though I hate how divided we are. I hate the stories that I hear about our family hating one another. I miss Granddaddy Lewis. I felt like he was the glue that held the family together, and ever since he died everybody pretty much went their separate ways with their families (even though we are all family). I wish we could all get along because there's nothing like a family that loves one another and takes care of one another. I miss when we were little how we always had family gatherings for no reason. We got to play and know all of our cousins. Now everyone is so distant, who knows who is who as far as family."

-KeYana Russell, *Retired U.S. Marine*

"The first albino I met was Travis and Jason. I really didn't feel no type of way because I didn't judge them or look at them funny. I thought they were cool and regular people. I don't judge people and I treat everybody the same. The Lewis family is cool with me. I don't have any problems with them."

-Sandy Thomas, Co-*Worker*

"I didn't get her name, but she was a regular customer of a restaurant I was managing. I thought she was kind of different — as far as her looks. And I couldn't figure out why, until someone told me it was because she's albino. I thought to myself, 'Oh, cool.' I was surprised and I am usually surprised because I don't often see an albino person. I try to get to know everyone I meet."

-**Peter Lao,** *Bookseller*

THE FAM
Chapter Eight

As you have read, the Lewis family is extremely full of life, love, and stories. I mean really, if the Lewis family had a reality TV show, it would definitely have you tuned in with laughs and scored as number one in highest ratings. Now we're not crazy; we just love to enjoy life and have fun. Not everyone knows how to handle a good family.

Some of the people we've let into our lives early on, I guess, did not understand or know how to handle the love we gave, so they have used and abused all that we offered. Our kindness was surely taken for granted.

Today we are cautious of people and situations that come around us. We have learned from our past mistakes and we've learned how to talk things over with each other to avoid those mistakes from happening again. And in doing so, we continually have a great life, with lots of love, and stories that are healed with laughter.

Let's talk about Life, Love & Stories.

LIFE: The ability to grow, change, advance ourselves, and so on. This family is one of the strongest families who knows how to come together in times of need. We always keep a helping hand out to take care of ourselves as a family. Times when my mother gets ill, we all see that it's coming, so we let each other know, and especially our father. "Let's keep an eye on Mama before it gets worse." We change course and each of us steps in and helps out while Mama is in the hospital. Life is hard and very complicated. When things in life shift on us, we have to know how to manage the change, even when the change is unexpected. I believe God always warns us of many things. It is up to us to acknowledge the signs, so we can't always say that something happened unexpectedly.

Another thing in life is *FAITH. According to the American Heritage Dictionary, Faith is a* confident belief in the truth, value, or trustworthiness of a person, idea, or thing. The biggest tool to recognize in life is faith, especially your own faith. Your faith is your own, and nothing or no one can take that away from you. No human being can steal your faith. Faith is what keeps you going. Receive it, keep it, trust it, believe it, own it, and, most importantly, use it. We don't need to physically climb any mountain. That is wasting too much unnecessary energy. The Bible tells us that we have the authority to speak to our mountains and they shall be moved.

One more important tool in life is *PATIENCE:* A bearing or enduring pain, difficulty, provocation, or annoyance with calmness. On a religious note, everybody wants a quick blessing from God, but few want to take time to put in work for the blessing. God has the whole world to take care of and not just you and your family. So just be patient and wait, wait *YOUR* turn.

LOVE: A feeling of strong or constant affection for a person. Love gets complicated only if you let it get there. For those who believe in love, just know that it conquers all: for better or for worse, for richer or for poorer, and in sickness and in health; love conquers all. The Lewis family, we don't verbalize "I love you" as much as we should, but we are more of expressers when it comes to giving or showing love. We argue, we fight, but before the day is over with, we fill in that gap by talking through our situations and show how much we love each other to make that gap whole again.

While interviewing a couple of people for this project, I could tell that I brought up a lot of mixed emotions in their minds. I know they miss the caring and love the Lewis's gave them with open arms.

STORIES: An account or recital of an event or a series of events. Stories are wonderful memories. Whether they are good or bad, somewhere in that story something or someone made you smile or laugh. If you want to feel better about something, just think of a story.

Recognize your own purpose.

Recognize why you are here. Yes we are here to serve God, but what does God want you to do for a living? How will you survive? How will you survive after you have recognized who God is? Recognize your own purpose and live your own life. Take responsibility for yourself.

FINAL THOUGHTS

As I stated in chapter 8, it is very important to recognize your own purpose. No matter who or what you are — your color, your race — just be who you are. Just be you.

When I took time to pray and asked God to reveal to me my purpose, I had to wait patiently. I had to hold on to my faith that he heard my prayer.

Life for ourselves isn't as hard as we make it out to be. I believe you'll have greater, easier days if you put God first in everything positive you do. Try testing your human spirit by God's Spirit, then tell me your outcome.

If you can sing a song about having no worries, prove it.

Remember to ask, be patient, recognize it, receive it, and then act on it.

Life is what you make it.

THANK YOU

I give all honors to God and His Son, our Lord and Savior Jesus the Christ. With God, all things are possible. As I had spoken my letter to God, in Jesus' name, it was my stamp to get it up to God's ear.

FACTS AND KNOWLEDGE OF ALBINISM

Knowledge of Albinism

Section 1
Signs, Symptoms, and Types of Albinisms

While most people with albinism have very light skin and hair, not all do. Oculocutaneous (pronounced ock-you-low-kew-TAIN-ee-us) albinism (OCA) involves the eyes, hair and skin. Ocular albinism (OA), which is much less common, involves primarily the eyes, while skin and hair may appear similar or slightly lighter than that of other family members.

Over the years, researchers have used various systems for classifying oculocutaneous albinism. In general, these systems contrasted types of albinism having almost no pigmentation with types having slight pigmentation. In less pigmented types of albinism, hair and skin are cream-colored and vision is often in the range of 20/200. In types with slight pigmentation, hair appears more yellow or red-tinged and vision may be better. Early descriptions of albinism called these main categories of albinism "complete" and "incomplete" albinism. Later researchers used a test that involved plucking a hair root and seeing if it would make pigment in a test tube. This test separated "ty-neg" (no pigment) from "ty-pos" (some pigment). Further research showed that this test was inconsistent and added little information to the clinical exam.

Recent research has used analysis of DNA, the chemical that encodes genetic information, to arrive at a more precise classification system for albinism. Four forms of OCA are now recognized – OCA1, OCA2, OCA3 and OCA4. Some are further divided into subtypes.

- Oculocutaneous albinism type 1 (OCA1 or tyrosinase-related albinism) results from a genetic defect in an enzyme called tyrosinase (hence 'ty' above). This enzyme helps the body to change the amino acid tyrosine into pigment. (An amino acid is a "building block" of protein.) There are two subtypes of OCA1. In OCA1A, the enzyme is inactive and no melanin is produced, leading to white hair and very light skin. In OCA1B, the enzyme is minimally active and a small amount of melanin is produced, leading to hair that may darken to blond, yellow/orange or even light brown, as well as slightly more pigment in the skin.

- Oculocutaneous albinism type 2 (OCA2 or P gene albinism) results from a genetic defect in the P protein that helps the tyrosinase enzyme to function. Individuals with OCA2 make a minimal amount of melanin pigment and can have hair color ranging from very light blond to brown.

- Oculocutaneous albinism type 3 (OCA3) is rarely described and results from a genetic defect in TYRP1, a protein related to tyrosinase. Individuals with OCA3 can have substantial pigment.

- Oculocutaneous albinism type 4 (OCA4) results from a genetic defect in the SLC45A2 protein that helps the tyrosinase enzyme to function. Individuals with OCA4 make a minimal amount of melanin pigment similar to persons with OCA2.

Researchers have also identified several other genes that result in albinism with other features. One group of these includes at least eight genes leading to Hermansky-Pudlak Syndrome (HPS). In addition to albinism, HPS is associated with bleeding problems and bruising. Some forms are also associated with lung and bowel disease. HPS is a less-common form of albinism but should be suspected if a person with albinism shows unusual bruising or bleeding.

- Skin Problems

Most people with albinism are fair in complexion. Skin or hair color is not diagnostic of albinism. People with many types of albinism need to take precautions to avoid damage to the skin caused by the sun. They should wear sunscreen lotions, hats and sun-protective clothing.

- Vision Problems

People with albinism always have problems with vision (not correctable with eyeglasses) and many have low vision. The degree of vision impairment varies with the different types of albinism and many people with albinism are "legally blind," but most use their vision for many tasks including reading and do not use Braille. Some people with albinism have sufficient vision to drive a car. Vision problems in albinism result from abnormal development of the retina and abnormal patterns of nerve connections between the eye and the brain. It is the presence of these eye problems that defines the diagnosis of albinism. Therefore the main test for albinism is simply an eye examination.

Section 2
Genetics

The genes for OCA are located on "autosomal" chromosomes. Autosomes are the chromosomes that contain genes for our general body characteristics, contrasted to the sex chromosomes. We normally have two copies of these chromosomes and the genes on them – one inherited from our father, the other inherited from our mother. Neither of these gene copies is functional in people with albinism.

However, albinism is a "recessive trait." So, even if only one of the two copies of the OCA gene is functional, a person can make pigment, but will carry the albinism trait. Both parents must carry a defective OCA gene to have a child with albinism. When both parents carry the defective gene (and neither parent has albinism) there is a one in four chance at each pregnancy that the baby will be born with albinism. This type of inheritance is called "autosomal recessive" inheritance.

Ocular albinism (OA1) is caused by a genetic defect of the GPR143 gene that plays a signaling role that is especially important to pigmentation in the eye. OA1 follows a simpler pattern of inheritance because the gene for OA1 is on the X chromosome. Females have two copies of the X chromosome while males have only one copy (and a Y chromosome that makes them male). To have ocular albinism, a male only needs to inherit one defective copy of the gene for ocular albinism from his carrier mother. Therefore almost all of the people with OA1 are males. Indeed, parents should be suspicious if a female child is said to have ocular albinism.

For couples who have not had a child with albinism, there is no simple test to determine whether a person carries a defective gene for albinism. Researchers have analyzed the DNA of many people with albinism and found the changes that cause albinism, but these changes are not always in exactly the same place, even for a given type of albinism. Moreover, many of the tests do not find all possible changes. Therefore, the tests for the defective gene may be inconclusive.

If parents have had a child with albinism previously, and if that affected child has had a confirmed diagnosis by DNA analysis, there is a way to test in subsequent pregnancies to see if the fetus has albinism. The test uses either amniocentesis (placing a needle into the uterus to draw off fluid) or chorionic villous sampling (CVS). Cells in the fluid are examined to see if they have an albinism gene from each parent.

For specific information and genetic testing, seek the advice of a qualified geneticist or genetic counselor. The American College of Medical Genetics and the National Society of Genetic Counselors maintain a referral list. Those considering prenatal testing should be made aware that people with albinism usually adapt quite well to their disabilities and lead very fulfilling lives.

Section 3
Treatment, Vision Rehabilitation

Eye problems in albinism result from abnormal development of the eye because of lack of pigment and often include:

- Nystagmus: regular horizontal back and forth movement of the eyes

- Strabismus: muscle imbalance of the eyes, "crossed eyes" (esotropia), "lazy eye" or an eye that deviates out (exotropia)

- Photophobia: sensitivity to bright light and glare

- People with albinism may be either far-sighted or near-sighted and usually have astigmatism

- Foveal hypoplasia: the retina, the surface inside the eye that receives light, does not develop normally before birth and in infancy

- Optic nerve misrouting: the nerve signals from the retina to the brain do not follow the usual nerve routes

- The iris, the colored area in the center of the eye, has little to no pigment to screen out stray light coming into the eye. (Light normally enters the eye only through the pupil, the dark opening in the center of the iris. But in albinism, light can pass through the iris as well.)

For the most part, treatment of the eye conditions consists of visual rehabilitation. Surgery to correct strabismus may improve the appearance of the eyes. However, since surgery will not correct the misrouting of nerves from the eyes to the brain, surgery will not improve eyesight or fine binocular vision.

In the case of esotropia or "crossed eyes," surgery may help vision by expanding the visual field (the area that the eyes can see while looking at one point).

People with albinism are sensitive to glare, but they do not prefer to be in the dark, and they need light to see just like anyone else. Sunglasses or tinted contact lenses help outdoors. Indoors, it is important to place lights for reading or close work over a shoulder rather than in front.

Various optical aids are helpful to people with albinism and the choice of an optical aid depends on how a person uses his or her eyes in jobs, hobbies, or other usual activities. Some people do well using bifocals which have a strong reading lens, prescription reading glasses, or contact lenses. Others use hand-held magnifiers or special small telescopes and some prefer to use screen magnification products on computers.

Some people with albinism use bioptics, glasses which have small telescopes mounted on, in, or behind their regular lenses, so that they can look through either the regular lens or the telescope. Newer designs of bioptics use smaller lightweight lenses. Some states allow the use of bioptic telescopes for driving.

Optometrists or ophthalmologists who are experienced in working with low vision patients can recommend various optical aids. Clinics should provide aids on trial loan and provide instruction in their use. The American Foundation for the Blind maintains a directory of low-vision clinics. In Canada, support is available from the Canadian National Institute for the Blind.

Section 4
Medical Problems

In the United States, most people with albinism live normal life spans and have the same types of general medical problems as the rest of the population. The lives of people with Hermansky-Pudlak Syndrome can be shortened by lung disease or other problems. Other conditions include Chediak-Higashi and Griscelli Syndrome.

In tropical countries, those who do not use skin protection may develop life-threatening skin cancers. If they use appropriate skin protection, such as sunscreen lotions rated 20 SPF or higher and opaque clothing, people with albinism can enjoy outdoor activities even in the summer. People with albinism are at risk of isolation because the condition is often misunderstood. Social stigmatization can occur, especially within communities of color, where the race or paternity of a person with albinism may be questioned.

Families and schools must make an effort not to exclude children with albinism from group activities. Contact with others with albinism or who have albinism in their families or communities is most helpful. NOAH can provide the names of contacts in many regions of the country.

Section 5
Society and Culture

Society's attitudes about albinism have a tremendous influence on the person with the condition. These influences will vary from person to person and at different stages of life. Having albinism also has a tremendous emotional impact on people. That also varies from person to person and at different stages of their lives. It is in the balance and interplay between the external world and each individual's internal response that a sense of self is born and sustained. Albinism is an important part of that sense of self.

The First Influence: A Disability or Not?

Neither the general public nor those with the condition agree about whether to identify albinism as a disability. This ambiguity creates a problem in the language used to talk about the condition. It also makes it difficult for those with albinism to identify themselves as a group. In many ways, albinism is unique. That uniqueness, however, leads to separateness and isolation for many people. Social attitudes toward albinism are often similar to those experienced by other disability and minority groups. These attitudes include a lack of understanding, fear of the unknown, and prejudice based on appearance.

The Americans with Disabilities Act defines disability with respect to an individual as "a physical or mental impairment that substantially limits one or more of the major life activities of such individual; a record of such an impairment; or being regarded as having such an impairment." Since albinism involves a visual impairment, some people consider it a disability. One definition of handicap is "the obstacles a person encounters in the pursuit of goals in real life, no matter what their source." Thus a person with a disability may be handicapped in pursuing the life he wants to live.

The identification of albinism as a disability is complicated by the concept of legal blindness. In the United States, a person is legally blind if his or her vision cannot be corrected with glasses or contacts to better than 20/200 in his or her better eye. By this standard, some with albinism fit the legal category of visual impairment and some do not. Yet, in spite of varying visual acuity, many of the problems experienced by those with albinism remain similar.

The Second Influence: Physical Appearance

The first aspect of albinism which most people notice is the person's unusual appearance. The white hair and skin of oculocutaneous albinism are powerful factors from birth. The new baby will often be much lighter in color than any family member. In non-white races, the coloring of the baby with albinism is a dramatic contrast to the family and community. Color has been a highly charged characteristic in our culture historically. Strangers will often make unwanted and unkind comments about the appearance of a child.

Beyond color, a child's eyes may be moving rapidly and not focusing together. The child may have to squint, tilt his or her head, and hold things close in order to see. Children with albinism often use glasses and optical aides to enhance their vision. Therefore the child with albinism often feels isolated not only in physical appearance but also in the conduct of everyday life.

This perception of being different can lead to an immense effort to act as much like "normal" as possible.

A person with albinism can feel a lot of pressure, both from themselves and from other people, to minimize the differences albinism causes. This effort can result in a great deal of stress for a person continually trying to maximize visual ability. The pressure can even lead a person with albinism to deny entirely that he or she has albinism, thereby losing touch with a very important aspect of one's identity.

Family and close friends can counter this isolation and denial. Being prized and valued as a whole person is the foundation for a lifetime of self-esteem and inner strength. This prizing must include an honest acknowledgment and acceptance of the condition of albinism. It is vitally important that families can freely discuss the impact of albinism in each of their lives.

The Third Influence: Language, Myth, Stereotype

Language can shape ideas and create reality. The word "albino" is commonly used in many languages, including English. Some people are comfortable with the word and prefer being called an albino. However, people often use the word "albino" in hurtful ways. Many feel it is dehumanizing to refer to a person in terms of a condition. Although slightly cumbersome, the terms "person with albinism" and "people with albinism" put the person first and the condition second.

Teasing and name-calling are other ways in which language can be very dehumanizing. Almost all children face teasing during their school years and they need to develop positive coping strategies. Parents, teachers and increased education about albinism can help with this problem. Throughout the world, people have misconceptions about albinism, ranging from notions that people with albinism have magical powers to the belief they are retarded. Among African-Americans, a common myth is that babies with albinism result from a union between an African-American woman and a Caucasian man.

Another common myth is that people with albinism must have red eyes. People with albinism usually have blue or gray eyes which sometimes appear reddish in certain types of light. Sometimes, myths are so widespread even the person with albinism believes them.

The media, including literature and film, have contributed to stereotypes of albinism. The character with albinism is often portrayed as villainous, deviant, supernatural or sadistic. Also some news reports and encyclopedia articles have included false or incomplete information about albinism. It is difficult for the public to know what is true vs. untrue.

The Fourth Influence: The Family

It is vital that the family have accurate information about albinism. New parents need support and time to understand the condition of their child. Parents and family members may need to face some unpleasant stereotypes they have learned about albinism. Siblings need to understand why their brother or sister looks different and why they seem to be getting so much attention. There is no single force greater than the family in helping a child understand and accept himself or herself.

The Emotional Component of Albinism

Along with the external influences of society, every person has a vital and essential emotional response to his or her personal experiences with albinism. These responses shape who we are and how we adapt to albinism. A strong emotional response is a normal part of living, growing, and intellectual development. Suppressed emotions, on the other hand, often turn inward and cause stress, depression and physical maladies. Emotional responses to albinism will occur throughout life because of the many challenges and frustrations the condition presents and the many societal influences already mentioned.

It is very important to develop healthy ways to express and integrate these emotions. First, it is necessary to recognize feelings and determine their source. Parents can help children label the feeling the child feels, then help the child connect that feeling to a specific reason or event. For example, a parent might say, "I know you're sad because you have to put on sunscreen before you go swimming." Then the parent can help the child "do" something with the emotion such as talking about it, playing, yelling, running, crying — whatever physical outlet it takes to release the feeling. This validation and release are essential in processing an emotion.

Adults with albinism can go through this process by having friends and family listen to their frustrating, discouraging, or proud experiences.

Some ways to release an emotional charge are physical activity, taking action in the form of education or advocacy, journal and letter writing, or doing something that is self-nurturing. Sometimes professional help from a therapist or counselor can assist a person work through the highly charged issues of albinism. Coping with albinism often isn't easy. However, working through the issues albinism causes not only leads to great personal satisfaction, but also to a greater understanding of human kind.

Conclusions

A very basic human need is to be "seen" by another person — to be known and accepted. This is poignantly true for the person with albinism who may be immediately "noticed" by many, but truly "seen" by few. This explains why it feels like a hidden condition despite its obviousness. Being involved with others is a way to decrease isolation and share in the combined knowledge and experience of the group. It is a way to gain confidence and strength in meeting the challenges of this condition.

Albinism, often unexpected in a family, can be a catalyst for acceptance, understanding, and love that encompasses all family members and each of their individual differences. It is a physical manifestation of uniqueness, with unique joys and hardships. Through the efforts of dedicated families and individuals, albinism is becoming known and understood.

Coping with easing and Name-Calling

Many parents said teasing, insensitivity, and ignorance about albinism were their greatest challenges. The young people reported being called names like "Whitey," "Snow White," "Casper," "Four Eyes," "Blind Eyes," "Grandma," and "Grandpa." They were asked why their heads shake, whether they pour bleach all over themselves, and other embarrassing questions. They also reported being excluded from games because they weren't "good enough."

I, too, experienced many of these same things. I was asked once if I could see in the dark. Another time a complete stranger walked up behind me and demanded that I look at her. I think she wanted to look at my eyes.

Understanding this behavior is one of the first steps in learning to deal with these experiences yourself or to help your child cope with albinism. What makes children (and others) tease and engage in name-calling? What causes the crude remarks, the callous behavior and the insensitive questions? One reason may be fear. Ancient people believed that to name something was to control it. We know today that people can be controlled by repetitious name-calling when they begin to believe the name, and act according to that label. Other reasons for name-calling, teasing and insensitivity are lack of knowledge, curiosity, a genuine desire to learn, and an inability to express questions constructively.

Albinism is *Hot!*

Some people tease in order to get to know another person better or to express affection. This kind of teasing usually isn't hurtful. However, if the person being teased doesn't have a positive self-image, and isn't comfortable with albinism, even affectionate teasing can hurt.

First, develop a positive self-image and attitude toward albinism. Add to that a thorough knowledge of albinism itself and you'll find yourself becoming more comfortable when discussing it with others. The standard "dumb" questions can become opportunities for education if one has self-confidence.

Parents can help their children deal with the hurtful comments by encouraging them to share their experiences and their feelings about them. Parents can also help their children by exploring new, positive ways to respond to the teasing and name-calling in the future and by practicing through role playing. Sometimes presenting information in class about albinism can reduce the amount of teasing and name-calling. Parents or the student can make the presentation, depending on the circumstances. Parents may need to educate the teachers first.

Schools should teach kids that hurtful behavior toward people with any sort of difference is a form of discrimination. A series of lessons on disabilities can provide information about albinism in the context of a variety of disabilities and other differences. Videos, puppet shows such as Kids on the Block, and other materials can teach this lesson on a child's level.

N.O.A.H. *(National Organization of Albinism and Hypopigmentation)* **"What Is Albinism?" "Social Aspects of Albinism", 1995-2002. Web. 21 March 2013**

Persecutions

Persecutions of people with albinism are based on the belief that certain body parts they have can transmit magical powers. This superstition, which is present in some parts of East Africa, has been promulgated and exploited by witch doctors and others who use such body parts as ingredients in rituals, concoctions and potions with the claim that their magic will bring prosperity to the user ("muti" or medicine murder). As a result, people with albinism have been persecuted, killed and dismembered, and graves of albinos dug up and desecrated. At the same time, people with albinism have also been ostracized and even killed for exactly the opposite reason, because they are presumed to be cursed and bring bad luck.

Tanzania

It is estimated that more than 150,000 albinos live in Tanzania; 8,000 are registered with the Tanzania Albino Society (TAS). A number of albinos have fled to the Dar es Salaam area as they feel safer in an urban setting. Tanzania is thought to have the largest population of albinos in Africa. In December 2007 the Tanzania Albino Society accused the government of inactivity in the face of four albino killings over the previous three months. While older albino women with red eyes had been at risk for being murdered sporadically in the past as witches, this killing spree may have been the beginning of the ongoing persecution of albinos with the intent to harvest the victims' body parts.

With escalating killings, then-President Jakaya Kikwete publicly and repeatedly condemned witch doctors, their helpers and middlemen, and the clients, which include members of the police force, for these murders. Victims include children snatched or abducted from their parents. The killers and their accomplices use hair, arms, legs, skin, eyes, genitals, and blood in rituals or for witch potions. Fishermen incorporate albino hair into their nets in their hope to catch more fish from Lake Victoria or to find gold in the belly of the fish that they catch.

A number of steps were taken by the government to protect the albino population. The president ordered a crackdown on witch doctors in the spring of 2008.

In addition, an albino woman, Al-Shymaa Kway-Geer, was named to become a member of the parliament, the first albino in such a position in the history of Tanzania. Police have also been advised to generate lists of albinos and provide special protection for them. To foil grave robbers, graves of the albinistic were to be sealed with concrete. However, by October 2008, killings had not abated, and while some suspects had been apprehended, no convictions had taken place. It was estimated that over 50 murders had taken place since March 2007, many of them in the mining and fishing communities near Lake Victoria, especially at Mwanza, Shinyanga and Mara.

In January 2009, Prime Minister Mizengo Kayanza Peter Pinda had declared war on the albino hunters, and in an effort to stop the trade in albino body parts he had revoked the licenses of all the country's witch doctors that use the body parts in their black magic fetishes.

First Conviction

The first-ever conviction for the killing of an albino in Tanzania occurred on Sept. 23, 2009 at the High Court in Kahama. The conviction came about following the murder and mutilation of a 14-year-old boy, Matatizo Dunia, who was attacked by three men in Bukombe district in Shinyanga Region in December 2008. The men carried Dunia from his home late at night before chopping him into pieces. One of them was later found with Dunia's leg in his possession. The rest of Dunia's body parts were located concealed in shrubbery. The men confessed a desire to sell Dunia's parts to a witch doctor, yet despite this, their legal team had not anticipated the death sentence of hanging which the three men would receive.

Canada's Under the Same Sun albino activist organization praised the breakthrough, but its founder, Peter Ash, remarked, "This is one conviction. There are 52 other families still awaiting justice." The Tanzania Albino Society's chairman Ernest Kimaya called for the hanging to be made public to further demonstrate to others that the issue of killing albinos was to be taken seriously.

Other African States

By June 2008 killings had been reported in neighboring Kenya and possibly also the Democratic Republic of Congo. In October of that year AFP reported on the further expansion of killings of albinos to the Ruyigi region of Burundi. Body parts of the victims are then smuggled to Tanzania where they are used for witch doctor rituals and potions. Albinos have become "a commercial good," commented Nicodeme Gahimbare in Ruyigi, who established a local safe haven in his fortified house. By 2010 cases had also been reported from Swaziland.

International Reactions

After events involving murders of albino humans by three Tanzanian men had been publicized by the BBC and others, the European Parliament strongly condemned the killing of albinos in Tanzania on Sept. 4, 2008. The U.S. House of Representatives passed H. Resolution 1088, introduced by Rep Gerry Connolly (D, VA), by a vote of 418-1 on Feb. 22, 2010. The resolution condemns the attacks and killings, categorizes them as human rights violations, and urges the governments of Tanzania and Burundi to vigorously prosecute such cases and to conduct educational campaigns to combat the superstitious beliefs that underlie the violent attacks.

Wikipedia, The Free Encyclopedia. "Persecution of People with Albinism". 8 March 2013.

Web. 21 March

MORE ABOUT THE AUTHOR

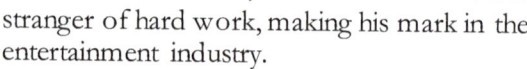

(Cedrick Shamar) Lewis, a native of Columbia, South Carolina and is no stranger of hard work, making his mark in the entertainment industry.

At age of 5, he found his love for music and began to find his own voice in singing. Recording artists who have inspired him the most are: R. Kelly, Marques Houston, Mariah Carey, Brandy and Monica.

In mid-2016, he begin works on his own music; a song called "#FEELINGS," which will be followed up by an EP album titled "Who's He?" Lewis is and actor and model and enjoys these gifts. During down time, he enjoys drawing.

In 2012, he recognized his purpose from God to become a certified *Author and Inspirational Speaker*. With stress and depression of giving up on this project, God's strength and encouraging words from family and friends allowed him to push through and proceed on with what God has told him to do.

Cedrick decided to write this book to introduce the word "Albinism", and to describe the characteristics of the word. He gives personal experiences that he and his family had gone through throughout life situations; from childhood into early adult years.

Currently he is *Leading Operating Manager* at The UPS Store. Working for two years plus with the franchise has helped him gain self-control and confidence in himself physically, mentally, and financially with future projects. It has also helped him give total care for his dog Codei; whom he rescued.

To know more about Cedrick Shamar and upcoming projects, friend him on Facebook and or follow him on Instagram:

@Cedrick Shamar via Facebook
@Cedrick Shamar via Instagram
-Recognize your own purpose: Be smart and be wise; work hard and always remain humble.
(Cedrick Shamar) Lewis

www.ingramcontent.com/pod-product-compliance
Lightning Source LLC
Chambersburg PA
CBHW042050290426
44110CB00001B/13